The Vestry Book of Kingston Parish

Mathews County, Virginia,

(until May 1, 1791, Gloucester County)

1679-1796

Transcribed, Annotated, and Indexed by

C. G. Chamberlayne

HERITAGE BOOKS
2011

HERITAGE BOOKS
AN IMPRINT OF HERITAGE BOOKS, INC.

Books, CDs, and more—Worldwide

For our listing of thousands of titles see our website
at
www.HeritageBooks.com

A Facsimile Reprint
Published 2011 by
HERITAGE BOOKS, INC.
Publishing Division
100 Railroad Ave. #104
Westminster, Maryland 21157

Originally published:
Old Dominion Press
Richmond, Virginia
1929

International Standard Book Numbers
Paperbound: 978-0-7884-1323-0
Clothbound: 978-0-7884-8881-8

The Vestry Book

OF

Kingston Parish

TO

DR. WILLIAM G. STANARD

SECRETARY OF THE VIRGINIA HISTORICAL SOCIETY,

in recognition of his extraordinary services and fruitful labors
in the field of historical investigation, whereby
he has made all serious students of
Virginia's history his debtors,
this volume is
with gratitude and great respect
Dedicated
by
The EDITOR

Preface

The MS. volume hereinafter reproduced contains the earliest records of Kingston Parish, Mathews County, Virginia, known to be in existence, though the parish itself can be traced back to the year 1657 [see page x], and was probably established as early as 1652. It is one of the many Vestry Books that Bishop Meade used as sources when writing his *Old Churches, Ministers and Families of Virginia,* and is now in the possession of the Library of the Theological Seminary of Virginia, at Alexandria. Permission to transcribe and publish it was given the undersigned by the Rev. Berryman Green, D. D., LL. D., Dean of the Seminary.

The "Vestry Book" is a folio 14 inches tall by 9 inches wide, and contains 61 leaves. It is, properly speaking, not one record, but two; but at what date the two manuscripts were bound up together is not known to the present editor. The first record begins with the year 1679 (Nov. 15), and ends in 1726; it consists of 6 leaves (12 pages). The second record starts with the year 1740(?), and ends in 1796; it comprises 55 leaves (110 pages). Lying in the book, but not attached to it in any way there was discovered a small sheet of paper, 6½ inches by 5¾ inches, containing a copy of an Order of Gloucester County Court, dated Feb. 5, 1784, directing the Vestry of Kingston Parish to divide the parish into precincts for processioning, etc. A transcript of this paper will be found on page 131.

In Meade, *Old Churches, Ministers and Families of Virginia,* Phil., 1885, Vol. I, p. 325, occurs under the heading "Kingston Parish, Mathews County", the following:

"This was originally one of the parishes in Gloucester.

There are loose leaves of an old vestry-book, going back to the year 1677, the first of which leaves do not indicate how much older the book was. It was called the parish in North River precinct. It has a peculiarity distinguishing it from all other parishes. With the vestrymen, who were generally very few, there met a larger number of the inhabitants, who seem to have managed the affairs of the parish in conjunction.

"From 1677 to 1691 the Rev. Michael Typerios and James Bowker were ministers; but when their ministries began or ended cannot be made out. In the year 1740 the Rev. John Blacknal appears on the first page of another imperfect vestry-book. It cannot be ascertained how much of the vestry-book was lost, and how long Mr. Blacknal may have been the minister before 1740. He died in 1747 and was succeeded by the Rev. John Dixon in 1750, the Rev. John Locke having served meanwhile for three months. In the year 1770 Mr. Dixon resigned, and died in 1777. Four applicants appeared for the parish, the Revs. Thomas Baker, Thomas Field, Arthur Hamilton, and Archibald Avens, of whom Mr. Field was chosen, Mr. Baker having previously served three months. In the year 1778, Mr. Field either dying or resigning, Revs. Robert Read and William Dunlop were candidates, when the former was chosen. In the year 1784 the Rev. Thomas Hopkinson became its minister, and in the year 1789 the Rev. James McBride. In 1794 the Rev. Armistead Smith, of the old family of Smith in that part of Virginia, became the minister, being ordained by Bishop Madison."

To the foregoing recited facts, all of which Bishop Meade found in the records of Kingston Parish embodied in the two old Vestry Books published in this volume, the editor can add little of importance. However, he hopes that the following notes containing extracts from various sources may prove of some interest to students of Colonial Virginia parish history.

In *Hening,* Vol. I, p. 371, under date Aprill the 26th 1652, occurs the following item, which contains, in the list of "the names of the several Burgesses returned by the Sherriff to this Grand Assembly", the first mention of Glocester County in *Hening:*

"Glocester County	Mr. Hugh Guinne Mr. Fra. Willis"

In *Hening,* Vol. I, pp. 373-375, under date November the 25th, 1652, occur the following items:

(1) "The names of the Burgesses for the severall Plantations.

Gloster County	Coll. Hugh Gwinne Mr. Fra. Willis."

(2) "WHEREAS Chr. Boyse by appeale from the Governour and Councill the last court impleaded Coll. Hugh Gwinne before this Grand Assembly about certain land in Pyancatannk River, The Assembly vpon pervsall of their severall pattents and grants doe finde prioritie of title for the said Gwinne, according to former orders in the government of Sr. William Berkeley, Knt. and the last quarter court, And the plt. & defendant to beare theire owne charges."

(3) "IN the difference between Mr. Peter Ranson, plt. and John Hewett and Wm. Holder, defend'ts. It is ordered by this Grand Assembly that Mr. Peter Ranson's pattent shall stand good for 1100 acres of land in Mock-Jack bay, And that Hewett and Holder be outed and decline the possession till it be made appeare void by some that shall make better right appeare, It now appearing that none pretending to it in the right of Dawber have power to question his title; 100 lb of tob'o being allowed him for costs from each of them (vizt) 100 lb. of tobacco from Holder, and 100 lb. of tobacco from Hewett, *alias* execution."

(4) "IT is ordered by the Grand Assembly, that Mr. Peter Ranson shall have and enjoy 1100 acres of Land in Mock-Jacks bay on the North River of Mock-Jacks bay on the easterne side thereof, and the other 500 acres being granted to Mr. Wm. Whitby being the first grantees by this Assembly."

On page 304 of Pattent Book 4 in the Virginia Land Office, State Capitol, Richmond, Va., occurs, under the date March 15, 1657, the record of a grant to John Chapman of 250 "Acres of Land in the County of Glouceſter in Kingston Parish upon the South side of Peanketank River."

In *Hening,* Vol. II, p. 552, under the date March 15, 1676-7 occurs the following item recounting the experiences suffered at the hands of Governor Sir Wm. Berkeley by one of the followers of Nathaniel Bacon, the Rebel, in Kingston Parish:

"Whereas Sands Knowles, of Kingston Parish in Gloucester county, being in rebellion against his majesty, was, in the month of October last, (then in the height of the late horrid rebellion) by virtue of a commission to major Robert Beverley, granted by the right honourable the governor, taken prisoner, and with him, divers of his goods, servants, slaves, provisions, and a shallop, seized, taken and carryed away by the said Beverley and the souldiers under his command, and presented to the right honourable the governour, then at the house of major. gen. John Custis, in Northampton county, on the Easterne shore; who, for the said Knowles his rebellious and treasonable practices, committed him to prison, and condemned all his said goods, servants, slaves, provisions, and boate, and ordered and disposed part of the same to be expended, sould, and layd out for provisions for his majesties souldiers, which was accordingly done, and gave the rest immediately to the said Beverley and his souldiers under his command for their incouragement and good service. And whereas the said knowles remains a prisoner, under bayle, to this day, to answer the crimes, rebellions and treasons by him committed against his most sacred majestie, and soe excepted out of the right honourable the governour's general pardon, bearing date the 10th of ffebruary 1676-7, and grounded upon his majesties most gracious proclamation of pardon; for the crimes, treasons and rebellions by him committed, humbly offering to renounce, acquitt, and discharge all right or claime of him the said Knowles, forever hereafter, to any or all the said goods, servants, slaves, boate or provisions, by the said Beverley, or any souldier with him, soe taken and carried away, acknowledging the same to be justly lost (by him) and forfeited forever; his said relinquishment of the said goods, &c. was ordered to be entered upon record; and the said Knowles his petition granted, and his acknowledgement and humble submission, in open court, put upon record, to the end the King's majesties most gracious pardon may be of full force and effect to him the said Knowles, and his remaining estate, he takeing the oath of obedience and giving good bond with securities for his future good behaviour.

In the *Minutes of the Council and General Court of Colonial Virginia,* 1622-1632, 1670-1676, appears, under the date, The 15th March 1676, the following:

Whereas Mr *George Seaten* of *Kingſtone* ℘ish in *Glouceſter* County one of his Maties Justices of ye Peace being in Rebellion Againſt his moſt Sacred Maty was in the time of the ſaid Rebellion on or about the beginning of *november* laſt taken priſoner by Major *Robt Beverley* & with him divers of his Goods & P)viſions, Seized & taken & Carried to the Right Honoble the Governor then Reſideing on the *Eastern Shore* who Com̄d the Said *Seaton* - - - & Condemned & diſpoſed his goods & p)viſions Soe Seized & - - - to the vſe & Incouragemt of his Maties Souldiers & - - - Remained Priſoner vnder Bayle fouer - - - to the ſaid *Seaton* was by order of the Rt Honoble the Governor Seized & marked with the broad Arrow Butt left in the houſe & Poſſeſſion of the ſaid *Seaton,* vntill Convenient time for their Remouevall *And whereas* the ſaid *Geo Seaton* did this day Make Humble Sute to the Court that he might Receive the Benefitt & mercy of his Sacred Maties moſt Gracious ℘don Praying for Releaſement of his Said foure hhds of Tobacco Soe Seized as aforeſaid and Submiſſively Relinquiſhing all Right Claime, Title or Intreſt to any the ſaid Goods Seized or Carried away by the Said *Beverley* or his Souldiers *This Court doth order & Adjudge* the Said Goods to be by Reaſon of their being taken & removed in time of Rebellion wholly Loſt & fforfeited, Butt By Reason the ſaid ffower hoggſheads of Tobacco were only vnder Seizure & not removed that therefore the Said Seaton may make free vſe of the Same vntill it Shall be determined by his Ma[tie] & Lords of his Hono[ble] Councill whether the same be not forfeited by Reaſon of the ſaid Seizure, notwithſtanding the Benefitt of his ma[ties] Gravious ꝑdon is vpon the Said *Seatons* Humble Petition Granted & Confirmed to him he takeing the oath of Obedience & giveing bond wth Sufficient Security for his future Good behavior."

In the *Executive Journals of the Council of Colonial Virginia,* Vol. I, pp. 23 and 24 occurs the following item:

"Middle Plantation May 25th 1682

Whereas It is represented that some ill disposed women in Gloucester County, doe persist in y[e] evil and notorious riots, spoiles and great abuses and damages of cutting up Tobacco plants, in direct opposition to Lawes and Statutes in the like case made and provided and in high contempt to y[e] Govern[rs] Proclamation and possitive orders for preventing and suppressing all riots and outrages of y[t] nature, & whereas It is signified that y[e] wife of Thomas Allman and y[e] wife of Richard Longest are móst notoriously active in ye aforementioned wickedness and y[t] y[e] s[d] Thomas Allman & Richard Longest doe refuse to find good security for y[e] good behaviour of y[e] wives of them y[e] said Thomas Allman & Richard Longest Its therefore resolved & Accordingly ordered y[t] L[t] Coll Jo[n] Armstead do forthwith cause y[e] wives of Tho: Allman & Richd Longest to be taken into safe custody & them securely to detain, & cause to appear before y[e] Govern[r] & Councel att Middle Plantation on y[e] 30th instant to answer to what shal be objected ag[t] them on his Majesties behalfe & to be proceeded ag[t] as by Law in y[e] like case is prescribed."

In the same volume occurs, on page 157, the following:

"Att a Councill held at James Citty Feb[ry] 18th 1690 [1690-91]

John Stephens Master of the Shipp Bristoll Merch[t] now in Mockjack Bay, giving an account that in this present Voyage to this Country on the 15th December last he mett with a small French Barque belonging to Rochell in France, and came then from Keyou, who had an English Man Prisoner aboard, who they took from the said Barke but having but few Men and None of them willing to goe either for England or Virginia in the said Barque onely tooke from her two Petteraroes [Pedreroes (small guns)] three Musquetts, about seven hundred pds of Shugar, some Parretts and Parraketoes some Oranges and about seven hundred Sows [sous] and soe let her goe, On Consideration whereof It is Ord'd that the said Stephens putt the Patteraroes and Musquetts on Shore for their Mas use at Mr Sands Knowle's Plantation in Glocester County, and the rest being of small value, most of the Shugar being spent at Sea, to take for the Incouragement of the Men belonging to the aforesaid Shipp."

In the *Journals of the House of Burgesses of Virginia*, 1727-1734, 1736-1740 (Vol. VI), page 189, occurs the following:

"*Wedneſday, September* 4, 1734.

A Petition of *Robert Bernard*, and *Charles Tomkies*, Gent. was preſented to the Houſe, and read; praying That Leave may be given to bring in a Bill, to dock the Intail of Two Hundred and Fifty Acres of Land, whereof the ſaid *Robert Bernard* is ſeiſed in Tail Male, in the Pariſh of *Petſworth*, in the County of *Gloceſter*, and Veſting the ſame in *Charles Tomkies;* and to ſettle Four Hundred Acres of Land, in the Pariſh of *Kingſtone*, in the County aforeſaid, whereof the ſaid *Charles Tomkies* is ſeiſed in Fee, of greater Value, upon the ſaid *Robert Bernard*, to the ſame Uſes, according to an Agreement made between them

Ordered, That Leave be given to bring in a Bill, according to the prayer of the ſaid Petition: And that Mr *Francis Willis*, Mr *Armistead*, Mr *Martin*, and Mr *Henry Willis*, do prepare and bring in the ſame"

In *Hening*, Vol. XIII (1789-1792), page 162, occurs the following:

"CHAP XLI

An act for dividing the county of Gloucester

(Passed the 16th of December, 1790)

SECT. 1. BE *it enacted by the General Assembly,* That from and after the first day of May next, the county of Gloucester shall be divided into two distinct counties, that is to say, all that part of the said county lying to the eastward of a line, to begin at the mouth of North river, thence up the meanders thereof to the mill, thence up the eastern branch of the millpond to the head of Muddy creek, thence down the said creek to Piankatank river, shall be one distinct county, and called and known by the name of Mathews, and the residue of the said county shall retain the name of Gloucester".

The foregoing references to Kingston Parish, or to individuals more or less connected with that parish, are all that the editor has been able to find in the Colonial Virginia records in Richmond. It is to be regretted that they are so scanty. For the history of the parish subsequent to the period embraced in this volume, the student is referred to Meade, *Old Churches, Ministers and Families of Virginia,* Vol. I, pp. 325-327.

With regard to the name of the incumbent of Kingston Parish from 1680 to 1687 a few words here will, perhaps, not be out of place.

It will be noted above that Bishop Meade speaks of the Rev. Michael Typerios as having been one of two ministers of Kingston Parish between 1677 and 1691. Now the transcriber is of the opinion (which he advances, he hopes, with modesty) that the name of the minister in question was Zyperus and not Typerios. In support of this opinion he refers, first, to the photograph copy of page 3 of the MS. vestry book (facing page 5 of the printed volume), where the *autograph* signature of the clergyman appears, and, second, to the fact that in the years 1667 and 1683 a Rev. Mr. Superias (or Superious)preached on occasion in Christ Church Parish, Middlesex County (the adjoining parish to Kingston), as we know from references to him to be found on pages 11 and 40 of *The Vestry Book of Christ Church Parish, Middlesex County, Virginia*, 1663-1767. The clerk of the vestry might easily have written Superias or Superious for the name Zyperus (which he must often have heard pronounced but had perhaps never seen written), but no ordinary man could conceivably confuse two names as unlike in sound as Typerios and Superias.

The speciment pages of the MS. used to illustrate the volume are reproductions of photographs made from the original by Dementi, of Richmond. It is hoped that they will prove of interest as illustrating peculiarities of handwriting before the year 1700 (pages 3, 4 and 5) and common forms of abbreviation of the period between 1683 and 1751, some of which cannot be accurately reproduced in print (pages 3, 4, 5 and 30), as well as for other reasons. On page 3 can be seen the autograph signature of the Minister in 1687, while on pages 4, 5 and 46 appear the autograph signatures of many of the Vestrymen and Inhabitants between 1687 and 1760.

Blanks in the MS. which were left by the Clerk to be filled in later but were never filled in are indicated in the printed volume by blank spaces. Gaps in the MS. resulting from tearing, rubbing, or other kinds of intentional or unintentional mutilation are indicated by blank spaces enclosed in brackets. Unintentional omissions in the MS. and all mistakes of whatever kind are, as far as was found possible, reproduced in the printed volume as made. The number of unintentional errors made was very great. Examples of some of the more glaring ones can be found on pages 58 (line 4; where the last name of Captain Gwyn Reade was omitted) and 92 (last line; where the character & was written for the proper name Ann).

Pages in the MS. are indicated in the printed volume by Arabic numerals enclosed in parentheses.

In the indexes the number of times a name or a topic occurs on a page is indicated by a small Arabic numeral above, and to the right, of the numeral indicating the number of the page.

Although the editor has read the proof four times, in every case using the original MS. as his guide, he is aware of the fact that in works of this kind some mistakes are inevitable. He hopes that the number of such mistakes is small. Any one wishing to check up on the work can do so by comparing the printed volume with the original MS. (in the Library of the Theological Seminary of Virginia, at Alexandria) or with the photostat copy of the original on file in the Archives Department of the Virginia State Library, in Richmond.

To his son, Edward Pye Chamberlayne, for material aid in preparing the indexes, and to Mr. Edwin L. Levy, of the Old Dominion Press, to whose helpful suggestions and unwearied interest the mechanical excellence of the book is entirely due, the editor wishes to acknowledge his great indebtedness.

If this volume serves to awaken further interest in the preservation and reproduction in print of the parish records of Colonial Virginia, the editor will feel more than repaid for his trouble in preparing it for the printer.

C. G. CHAMBERLAYNE.

Richmond, Virginia,
August 31, 1929.

The Vestry Book

...of...

Kingston Parish

Mathews County, Virginia, 1679-1796

[ ]e
Pish ye North At a meeting [ ] Vestrymen & [ ]
[ ]ver p^r^cinct Novemb^r^ ye 15th 1679

P^r^sent Coll Richd Dudley
Mr James Ranſon
Mr James Hill Vestrymen

Mr George Burge
Mr George Leſcaillet Neighbour [ ]
The mark I of Thomas Bayley ye Said [ ]
The mark DH of Daniell Hunter then p^r^sent

It was & is agreed y^t^ Whereas there hath beene diverſe Tymb^r^ Trees f[ ] & made uſe of for ye Reparacon of the North-River Chapell wch trees grew up [ ] ye Land of Mr Thomas Tabb & was more then amounted to ye Said Tabbs propor[ ] It is agreed, Ordered, Consented to, & Determined by ye S^d^ Vestry y^t^ on Condicon Sd Tabb shall fully remitt all Claimes for & Concerning all Timb^r^ already f[ ] of his for ye uſe afores^d^ that there shall be noe more tymb^r^ trees fallen up[ ] Lands of ye sd Tabb for ye tyme to come untill ye rest of ye Pishoners in t[ ] Courſe have contributed proportionably as much for yᵉ uſe aforesd as he yᵉ sd [ ] hath done already In witneſse whereof yᵉ Vestry of yᵉ pʳcint of yᵉ North-Ri[ ] Chappell aforesd have hereunto Sett their hands yᵉ day & Yeare above Specefie[ ]

Signed by yᵉ Vestry & Neighbourhood as abo[ ]
are Named
Vera Copᵃ Testᵗ George Axe C Vestry Kˡ [ ]
1679

Kingstone ℘ish yᵉ North River pʳcint — At a meeting of yᵉ Vestrymen & Inhabitants of yᵉ pʳcinct of North River Octobʳ yᵉ 14ᵗʰ 1680

Mʳ Mychaell Zyperus Clerg

Mʳ Sands Knowles	Mʳ George Leſcaillet
pʳsent Mʳ James Ranſon	Mʳ Jnᵒ Seayres
Mʳ George Burge	Thomas Bayley
Vestrymen	Inhabitan[ ]

Bought of Mʳ James Ranſon for yᵉ Chappels uſe a great Church Bible & two Larg Common prayer books cost 100[ ]ˡᵇ ᵗᵒ

Bought of Mʳ Jnᵒ Seayres a Chest to keepe yᵉ Sᵈ Books cost 1[ ]

Ordered by yᵉ full consent of yᵉ abovesd Vestry & Inhabitants yᵗ Mʳ James [ ] be payd out of yᵉ pʳcinct One thousand pds of Tobᵒ for a great Bible & two [ ] Common prayer Bookes for yᵉ uſe of yᵉ North-River Chappell & yᵗ he colle[ ] himselfe as Churchwarden

Ordered yᵗ Mʳ Jnᵒ Seayes be allowed for a Chest wᵗʰ a lock & key to it [ ] keepe yᵉ abovesd Bookes One hundred pds of Tobᵒ to be pd him this pʳsent Co[ ] by yᵉ Churchwarden of yᵉ abovesd pʳcinct

Ordered yᵗ Tho Clapp be pd five hundred pds of Tobᵒ & cask for keepin[ ] Cleane yᵉ Chappell & yᵉ Chappell Yard

Mᵈᵐ This Vestry book given by mʳ Jnᵒ Seayres for yᵉ uſe

of ye p^r^cinct of ye Nor[ ] River ye day of ye said Vestry
The Charge of ye Sd p^r^cinct being 1630^lb^ of Tob^o^ divided by 119 Tyth[ ]b[ ] 13^lb^ of Tob^o^ ℘ pole & 83 being ye fraction on ye Division is allowed [ ] to be 14^lb^ ℘ pole

Tes^t^ George Axe
1680

(2)
[ ] on At a Meeting of ye Vestrymen & Inhabitants
[ ] y^e^ of ye aforesaid ℘^r^cinct Novemb^r^ ye 2^d^ 1681
[ ]th River
[ ]cinct

	Mr Sands Knowles	Mr Jno Seayres
P^r^sent	Mr James Ranson	
	Mr George Burge	Mr Charles Jones
	Vestrymen	Inhabitants

Ordered y^t^ Charles Jones Churchwarden of ye North-River p^r^cinct Collect three pounds of Tobacco ℘ pole of each Tythable in ye Said p^r^cinct for ye paym^t^ of five hundred pounds of Tobacco & Cask this p^r^ſent yeare to Thomas Clapp for ye paines he taketh upon ye Chappell & Chappell-Yard but partly out of Charity to ye Said Clapp
The abovesd Vestrymen & Inhabitants have thought good to continue ye Said Thomas Clapp in his abovesd Imploym^t^ & to allow him ye aforesd quantity of tobacco

Tes^t^ George Axe Cl Vest. Kingston
1681

At a Meeting of ye Vestrymen & Inhabitants of ye Northern p^r^cinct ye 23th of November 1682

Wee ye Subſcrib^rs^, Veſtrymen & Inhabitants of ye abovesd p^r^cinct doe Ord^r^ Jno Billups Churchwarden of ye said p^r^cinct to Repaire or cauſe to be repaired ye Chappell belonging to ye said prcinct & wt ye said Billups is at Charge about ye said Work he bring in an Acct thereof aſ soone as he hath done ye Same at wch tyme ordr shall be taken to make him full Sattisfaccon accordingly

George Burge
George Leſcaillet
The mark of
Daniell ⳩ Hunter
The mark of
Thomas I Bayley

M: Zyperus
James Ranſone
Sands Knowles
Rich dudley Jur

[ ] stone [ ] [ ] At a Meeting of ye Vestrymen & Inhabitants of ye Northern prcinct ye 18th of Novembr 1682

Mr Sands Knowles
ꝑrsent Mr James Ranson
Mr George Burge

Mr George Lescaillet Inhabitant

Ordered yt Jno Billups Churchwarden of ye North River prcinct Collect 4lb of Tobo ꝑ pole of each Tythable in ye said prcinct for ye Satiſfaccon of Thomas Clapp for keeping of ye Chappell & ye Chappell Yard Cleane

Test George Axe Cl Vestry Kingstone
1682

(3)
Kingstone ꝑish North- ſſ River prcint

At a Meeting of ye Vestry & Inhabitants of North R[ ] prcinct Octobr ye 27th 1683

ꝑrsent

Mr James Ranson
Mr Sands Knowles
Mr George Burge
Mr Jno Billups
Vestrymen

Mr Robt Peyton
Mr Richd Dudley
Mr Ambroſse Dudley
Daniell Hunter
Tho: Bayley
Charles Jones
Inhabitants

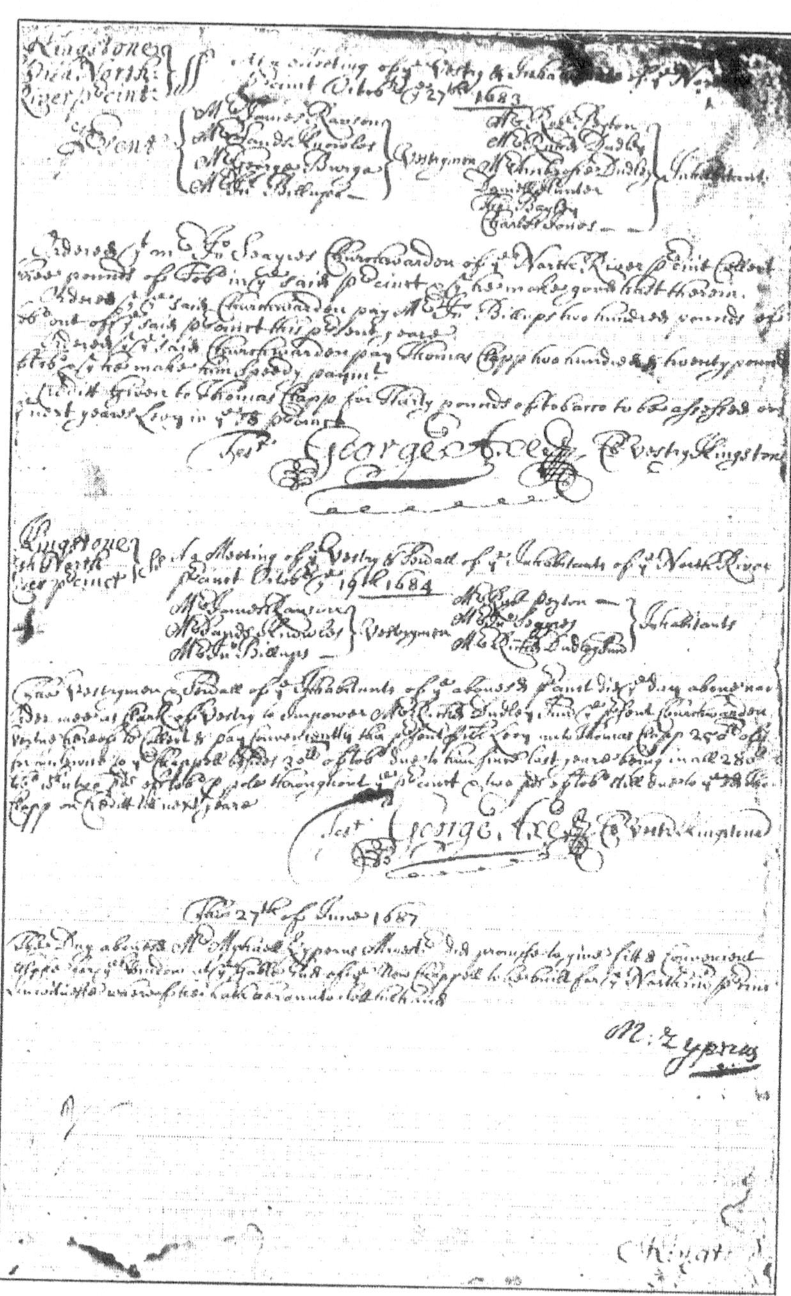

Page 3 of the Manuscript

Ordered y^t m^r Jno Seayres Churchwarden of y^e North River p^rcint Collect three pounds of Tob^o in y^e said p^rcinct & y^t he make good hast therein.

Ordered y^t ye said Churchwarden pay Mr Jno Billups two hundred pounds of tob^o out of ye said p^rcinct this p^rsent yeare.

Ordered y^t ye said Churchwarden pay Thomas Clapp two hundred & twenty pounds of tob^o & y^t he make him Speedy paym^t.

Creditt Given to Thomas Clapp for Thirty pounds of tobacco to be aſseſsed on ye next yeares Levy in ye sd p^rcinct

Tes^t George Axe Cl Vestry Kingstone

Kingstone ℘ish North River p^rcinct ſs At a Meeting of ye Vestry & Sevall of ye Inhabitants of ye North River ℘^rcinct Octob^r ye 19th 1684

Mr James Ranson
Mr Sands Knowles
Mr Jno Billups
Vestrymen

Mr Robt Peyton
Mr Jno Seayres
Mr Richd Dudley Jun
Inhabitants

The Vestrymen & Sevall of ye Inhabitants of ye abovesd p^rcinct did ye day above nam[ ] Order mee as Clark of Vestry to Impower Mr Richd Dudley Jun ye p^rſent Churchwarden [ ] Vertue hereof to Collect & pay Conveniently this p^rſent ℘ish Levy unto Thomas Clapp 250^lb of [ ] for his Service to ye Chappell beſides 30^lb of tob^o due to him ſince last yeare being in all 280^lb [ ] tob^o wch is two pds of tob^o ℘ pole throughout ye p^rcinct & two pds of tob^o still due to ye sd Tho[ ] Clapp on Creditt till next yeare

Tes^t George Axe Cl Vestr Kingstone

The 27th of June 1687

The Day abovesd Mr Mychaell Zyperus Minest^r did promiſe to give fitt & Convenient Glaſse for yᵉ Window at yᵉ Gable End of yᵉ New Chappell to be built for yᵉ Northern pʳcinc[ ]

In witneſse whereof he hath hereunto Sett his hand

M: Zyperus

Kingto[ ]

(4)

Kingstone Parrish North River ℘ʳcinct ſs — At a Meeting of yᵉ Vestrymen & Inhabitants of yᵉ abovesd yᵉ 11ᵗʰ of Octobʳ 1687

	Coll Richᵈ Dudley	Mʳ Richd Dudley
	Mʳ James Ranſon	Mʳ Ambroſe Dudley
℘ʳsent	Mʳ Sands Knowles	Mʳ Wᵐ Elliott
	Mʳ Jnᵒ Billups	Mʳ Tho: Neale
	Vestrymen	Mʳ Edd Sadler
		Inhabitants

Ordered by yᵉ abovesd Vestrymen & Inhabitants That Mʳ Robᵗ Elliott Churchwarden of yᵉ abovesd pʳcinct doe forthwith Collect of each Tithable ℘son in yᵉ sd pʳcinct 162ˡᵇ of good Sweet ſented Tobacco for & towards yᵉ building of a New Chappell in yᵉ above pʳcinct & for other Neceſsary Charges thereabout; And yᵗ yᵉ sd Churchwarden Satiſfye & pay unto Thomas Clapp for Cleaning yᵉ Chappell 276ˡᵇ of tobᵒ out of yᵉ sd Collection in Convenient Time to his Content & further yᵗ yᵉ sd Churchwarden Do detaine & Secure the Remaining Sum̃e of tobᵒ (after Collection thereof is made) in his hands, untill further ordʳ be Given him by yᵉ abovesd Vestrymen & Inhabitants at their next Meeting about their diſpoſeing thereof.

The Charg Levyed is as followeth vizᵗ

To Tobacco for yᵉ Workmen	20,000ˡᵇ Tobᵒ
To Tobᵒ for Glaſse	1,000
Tobacco for Cask	1080
To Tho Clapp	276
The Totall Sume is	22356 being

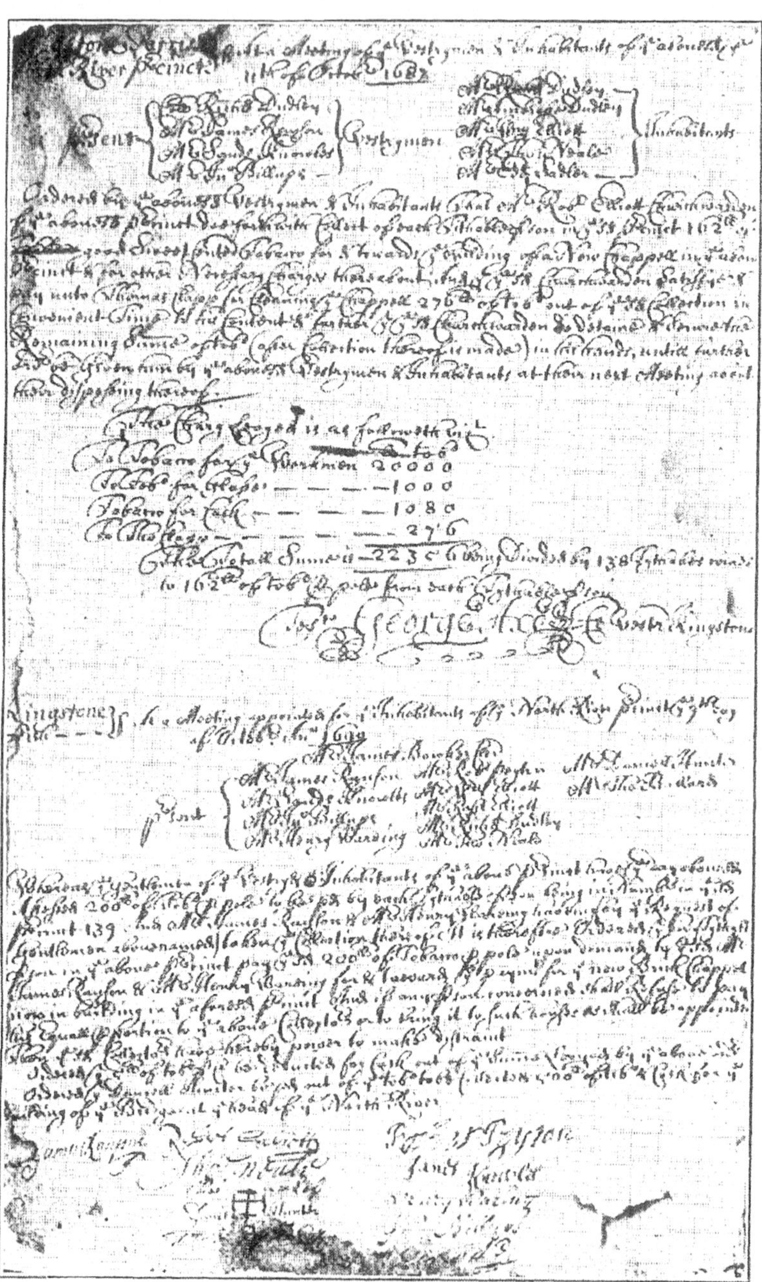

PAGE 4 OF THE MANUSCRIPT

Divided by 138 Tythables comes to 162lb of tob° ꝑ pole from each Tythable ꝑson

Test George Axe Cl Vestr Kingstone

Kingstone ꝑish ʃʃ At a Meeting appointed for ye Inhabitants of ye North River prcinct ye 9th day of October An° 1690

Mr James Boker Cler

	Mr James Ranʃon	Mr Wm Elliott
	Mr Sands Knowles	Mr Robt Elliott
prsent	Mr Jn° Billups	Mr Richd Dudley
	Mr Henry Wareing	Mr Tho Neale
	Mr Robt Peyton	Mr Daniell Hunter

Mr Tho Ballard

Whereas ye Gentlemen of ye Vestry & Inhabitants of ye above prcinct have ye day abovesd Aʃseʃsed 200lb of Tob° ꝑ pole to be pd by each Tythable ꝑson being in Numbr in ye sd prcinct 139 And Mr James Ranʃon & Mr Henry Wareing haveing (by ye Request of Gentlemen abovenamed) taken ye Collection thereof It is therefore Ordered yt evy Tythable ꝑson in ye above prcinct pay ye sd 200lb of Tobacco ꝑ pole upon demand to ye sd Mr James Ranʃon & Mr Henry Wareing for & toward ye paymt for ye new Brick Chappell now in building in ye aforesd ꝑrcinct And if any ꝑson concerned shall Refuʃe to pay the Equall ꝑportion to ye above Collectors or to bring it to ʃuch houʃes as Shall be appointed Then ye sd Collectors have hereby power to make diʃtraint

Ordered yt 5lb of tob° ꝑ Ct be deducted for Cask out of ye Sum̄e Levyed by ye above ordrs

Ordered yt Daniell Hunter be pd out of ye tob° to be Collected 500lb of tob° & Cask for ye building of ye Bridge at ye head of ye North River

James Ranſone	Robert Peyton
Robt Elliott	Sands Knowles
Tho: Neale	Henry Waring
The mark of	Jn° Billups
Daniell Hunter	[ ]m Elliott*
Thomas Ballard	

(5)

At ye aforesd Meeting ye Gentlemen then prsent did willingly Conſent yt there shall be [ ] to George Axe Clark for keeping of ye Vestry book & other paines by him taken at ye laying ye next Chappells Levy 500lb of tobacco & Cask

The Copy of Robt Trews Ingagmt

I Robt True in ye yeare 1689 have now Built ye North River Bridge, & have recd pay of Daniell Hunter these Lines shall be his diſcharg And further I doe oblige my Selfe mee my heires Execrs or aſsignes to ye Gentlemen of ye Vestry wth warranty to keep ye sd Bridge in good Repaire for ye full Tearme of Seaven yeares beginning from ye date above menconed as witnes my hand this prſent Moneth of December ye 21th 1690

Testes
George Gillett
Mathew Swanſone

The mark of
Robt True

Vera Copa Test George Axe Cl vestr Kingstone

Kingstone Parish
North River prcinct

At a Meeting of ye Vestrymen & Inhabitants of ye abovesd prcinct ye 19th day of Novembr 1691

Vestrymen	Inhabitants
Capt James Ranſone	Mr Robt Peyton
Capt Sands Knowles	Mr Richd Dudley
Capt Henry Waring	Mr Ambroſse Dudley
Mr Jn° Billups	Mr Wm Elliott
	Mr Daniell Hunter

* An illegible abbreviation follows this name. Probably it is Jnor (Junior).—C. G. C.

PAGE 5 OF THE MANUSCRIPT

Ordered y^t m^r Edmd Roberts pay unto George Axe Clark of y^e Vestry 500^lb of tob^o & Cask in y^e Northern ℘ecint this p^rſent Cropp

At a Meeting for y^e North River P^rcinct Octob^r ye 9th 1692

	Capt James Ranſone	Mr Wm Elliott
P^rsent	Capt Sands Knowles	Mr Thomas Ballard
	Mr Robt Peyton	Mr Hum: Tomkins
	Mr Jno Billups	Mr Tho: Neale

Ordered That Mr Robt Elliott Churchwarden Collect 138^lb of tob^o in ye North River p^rcinct of each Tythable ℘son there for ye Satisfaccon of m^r Edwd Malen ye last paym^t for building ye Chappell belonging to ye sd p^rcinct & for ye paym^t of Charles Sanders Sextone ye Sume of 300^lb tob^o for the Cleaning ye sd Chappell to this day & ye Remaind^r being 120^lb of tob^o to be pd to ye sd Sanders he giveing ye p^rcinc[ ] Creditt for it y^n next yeare

Ordered to m^r Edwd Malyn out of ye above tob^o to be Collected 18088^lb of Tob^o & Cask Saveing ſoe much as ye Churchwarden shall be out to finish what work is further to be done in ye Chappell

The Inhabitants of ye Above p^rcinct have given their free Conſent y^t Capt James Ranson to build a pew for his family in ye Chancell of ye Chappell

James Ransone	Robt Elliott
Sands Knowles	Rich dudley iuno^r
Robert Peyton	Thomas: Ballard
Jno Billups	John Butler
Wm Elliott*	Tho: neale

The mark of
W^m H Hurdle

* An illegible abbreviation follows this name. Probably it is Jno^r (Junior).—C. G. C.

(6)

rth River ꝑ^{r}cinct ʃʃ At a Meeting for ye aforesd ꝑ^{r}cinct ye 8th of Novemb^{r} 1693

Capt Sands Knowles Mr Robt Elliott
p^{r}sent Mr Jno Billups Inhabitants
Mr Wm Elliott Mr Tho: Ballard

Ordered to Charles Sanders one pound of Tob^{o} ꝑ pole in ye p^{r}cinct being in all 131^{lb} tob^{o} to be paid to ye Sd Sanders by ye Churchwarden of y^{t} p^{r}cinct

Charles Sanders is to give ye p^{r}cinct Creditt for 51^{lb} tob^{o} next yeare

Tes^{t} George Axe Cl vestry Kingst[ ]

Mr Edwd Maylen Dr Acc^{tt} 1692

To yor bill to Capt Ranson	2186
To yor note to Capt Peyton	2853
To yor note to Jno Butler	1700
To yor note to Capt Peyton	735
To yor note to Capt Knowles	975
To 2 hh^{ds} Tob^{o} yor boate foott*	1150
To tob^{o} p^{d} yo^{u} ꝑ Wm Robarts	600
To tob^{o} p^{d} Law: Parrott	30
To tob^{o} p^{d} m^{r} Axe ꝑ Seʃsions	70
To yor note to m^{r} Bayler	666
To tob^{o} p^{d} Burton ꝑ ꝑowell	133
To tob^{o} ꝑ 16846 at 5 ꝑ C^{t}	844
To tob^{o} due from m^{r} Gregory	1242
To yor note to Seʃsions	1300
To yor note to m^{r} Todd	1050
To tob^{o} p^{d} Tho: Hamon	169
To 3 hh^{ds} Tob^{o}	1860
	17563

* This word was difficult to decipher. It may be brott.—C. G. C.

To ball due to m^r Maylen 525

18088

℘ Contra C^r 1692

By yor Crd^t 18088

Recd ye abovesd Acc^tt this
19th of 7^ber 1693
℘ mee E^d Maylen

Tes^t Wm Robarts

This is a true Coppy of ye Acc^tt of ye last paym^t to m^r Edwd Maylen given mee by m^r Robt Elliott late Churchwarden of ye North River p^rcinct about ye Brick Chappell there lately finished

Tes^t George Axe Cl vestry

North River P^rcinct ſs At a Meeting for ye sd P^rcinct Octob^r ye 16th 1694

	Capt James Ranſone	Mr Richd Dudley
	Capt Sands Knowles	Mr Robt Elliott
p^rsent	Mr Jno Billups	Edm^d Roberts
	Mr Amb: Dudley	Humphry Tomkins
	Mr Wm Elliott	Wm Tomkins
		Inhabitants

There are 135 Tythables this year

Ordered y^t James Hill Churchwarden Collect one pound of Tob^o ℘ pole of each Tythable in [ ]^e above P^rcinct & pay ye Same to Charles Sanders who hath C^r for 14£ of tob^o ag^t next yeare

Ordered y^t ye Churchwarden pay 1080£ of good Tob^o to Capt James Ranſone who hath promiſed to give ye P^rcinct bills of Exchang for ye Same at 10^s ℘ C^t That therewith there may be bought a Pulpett Cloath & Cushion for ye Chappell belonging to ye above p^rcinct & y^t James Hill Churchwarden upon ye Rec^tt of ye sd Bills doe (wth ye first Conveniency) send for ye sd Ornamt of a Green Colour wth these letters underwritten wrought on ye Pulpett Cloath & yt ye sd Church warden diſcharg ye sd Capt Ranſone in ye behalfe of ye above prcinct upon ye Receipt of ye sd Bills of Exchang.

The Letters to be wrought on ye Pulpett Cloath are

x K x
x N x P x

Ordered yt ye above Churchwarden Collect Eight pounds of Tobo of Every Tythabl[ ] [ ]son in ye above prcinct for ye due ℘formance of ye aforesd Order

Test George Axe Cl vestr Kingsto[ ]

(7)

North River Prcinct — At a Meeting for ye Prcinct November ye [ ] 1695

prsent — Capt James Ranſone, Capt Sands Knowles, Mr Jno Billups — & other ye Inhabitants

Ordered yt Wm Tomkins Churchwarden Collect two pounds of Tobo ℘ pole of each Tythable in ye prcinct & pay ye Same to Charles Sanders for Cleaning ye Chappell

Charles Sanders is to give ye prcinct Creditt for 54£ Tobo ye next yeare

Test George Axe Cl vestr King [ ]

North River Prcinct — Att a Meeting for ye prcinct Octobr ye 4th 1696 ℘rsent The Vestrymen & Conſent of other ye Inhabitants

Ordered That Mr Wm Elliott Churchwarden Collect 1½£ tobo of each Tythable in ye above Prcinc[ ] & yt he pay to mr Shropshire 25£ tobo & to Charles Sanders 168£ tobo

Charles Sanders is to give ye Prcinct Creditt for 22£ tobo ye next Yeare

Test George Axe Cl vestry Kingstone

North River At ye North River Chappell ye 3d day of
℘rcinct ſs Novembr 1700

The Churchwarden of ye above prcinct was ye day & year aforesd Impowred to Collect one pound of Tobacco ℘ pole for to pay ye Sextone Jno Lucas there being 262 Tythables in yt Prcinct

Test George Axe Cl vestry King[ ]

To Humphry Tompkins
Churchwarden

North River Att A Meting for North River ℘cinct
℘cinct ſs October ye 17th 1701

℘sent ye Gent men of ye Vestry

Ordred that ye Church warden of ye Above ℘cinct doe forthwith Collect one pound of Tobaco: ℘ pole thro out [ ] Sd ℘cinct for ye payment of ye Sexton Thomas Neele & for to pay John Luckus 38lb of Tobaco which was de[ ] him last yeare Thare being this yeare within ye sd ℘cinct 149 tithables

To Henry Bolton Churchwardon
Test Henry Bolton Clr vestry Ki ℘ish

North River Att A Meeting Att ye North River Chapell
℘cinct ſs November ye 23d 1702

Capt: Ambros Dudly Vestry man

	Mr Richard Dudly	Mr Wm Elliott
℘sent	Mr James Ranson: Jur	Mr Robert Elliott
	Mr John Coott	Mr Wm Tomcins
	Mr Charles Jones	Mr Humphre Tomcins
		In habitants

Ordered that ye Church Wardin of ye Afore Sd ℘cinct doe forth with Collect two pounds of tobaco ℘ pole throu out ye S^d^ ℘cinct for ye payment of Thomas Neele Sexton: thare being dew to him upon Areares 109^lb^ tobaco & this ℘sent yeares Alowance 200^lb^ tob^o^—which is in all 309^lb^ tob^o^: thare being With in ye S^d^ ℘cinct this ℘sent yeare 180 tithables which being Aseased 2^lb^ ℘ pole Cuns to 360^lb^ tobaco The Remainer being 51^lb^ tob^o^ the S^d^ Church Wardin is to keepe in his hands & be Accountable for to ye S^d^ ℘cinct Next yeare

Ver^a^: Cop^a^: Test Henry Bolton Cl^r^ Vestry Kingsto ℘ish
To Henry Bolton Church Wardin
for North River ℘cinct

(8)

[ ] River Att A Meeting at ye North River
[ ]ll ʃs Chap[ ] ctob[ ] [ ]

℘sent Left^t^ Coll^o^ James Ranson
Capt Ambros Dudley Vestry Men
Mr Wm Elliott
Mr Robert Elliott
Mr Richard Dudley
Mr Humphry Tompcins Inhabetants

Ordered that y^e^ ℘sent Churchwarden do forth with Collect one pound of Tobacco ℘ pole of Each tithable ℘son within ye S^d^ ℘cinct for ye payment of ye Sexton there being with in ye S^d^ ℘cinct this ℘sent yeare 171 Tithables

Test Henry Bolton Cl^r^ Vy
℘

North River Chaple ʃs At A Meeting at ye Chaple aforesd on the firs day of November 1704

℘sent Vestry M Coll James Ransone
Capt Ambros Dudley
Mr Wm Elliatt
Mr Robert Elliott
Mr Richard Dudley
Mr Wm Tompcins
Mr Thomas Peyton
Inhabitants

It was this day Concluded on by ye Gen^{t} Men above saide for to Levey Tobacco for ye Repairing of ye Chaple afore sd which was accordenly done in manner following

[ ]dered	lb Tobacco
To pay for the shingles being 11000 att 15^{s} ℘ thousand	1650
To pay Wm Creedle for Covering ye sd Chaple	1300
To pay for 11000 Nayles	385
To Sallery & Cask att 13 ℘cent	433
To pay Thomas Neele Sexton	200
	3968

The S^{d} Som of 3968^{lb} Tobacco being Leveied through ye S^{d} ℘icnct Coms to 23^{lb} ℘ pole there being in ye S^{d} ℘cinct this ℘sent yeare on whome this is Levied 172 Tithables

Tes^{t} Henry Bolton Cl^{r} Vestry Kingston ℘ish

An accot of the Disposing of ye a bove S^{d}: 3968^{lb}: of Tob^{o}

To Shingls & Nailes	1574		
To More Nailes	123		
To Wasting	136 in ye 2 H^{h} sold to Capt Lewes		
To ye Carpenters Worck	1300		
To Wastedg	168 in ye 2 H^{h} p^{d} ye Carpenter		
To Sallery & Cask	433		
To ye Sexton	200		
To Stoped by ye Carpenter W^{m} C^{r}	018	Debt^{r} Side is	3968
		Cont^{r} C^{r} is	3964
	3952		
To Credett to ye Church-warden	12		
	3964		

Test Henry Bolton Cl^{r} vestry Ki[ ]

(9)

North River ℘cinct ʃs Att A Meeting for ye S^{d} ℘cinct on ye 24th of Novmber 1705

	Capt Ambros Dudley	Vestry Man
	Mr William Elliott	
	Mr Robert Elliott	
℘sent	Mr Richard Dudley	In Habitants
	Mr James Ransone S^r	
	Mr William Tompcins	
	Mr Thomas Peyton	

Ordered that Capt Ambros Dudley Church Worden doe forth with Collect 2^lb of Toba[ ] ℘ pole of Each Tithable ℘son within ye S^d ℘cinct for ye Satisfaction of ye Sexton & to pay for 100 foot of Planck for ye use of ye Chapell; there being in ye S^d ℘[ ] this ℘sent yeare 172 tithes which Cums to 344^lb Tobacco

Ordered To pay Mr Neele Sexton	200
To pay for planck	100
	300

Mor Credett due 44^lb Tob^o

Test Henry Bolton Cl^r vestry Kison ℘

North River
℘cinct 1706

Ordered that Coll James Ransone Churchwarden doe Collect One pound of Tobacco ℘ pole of Each tithable ℘son within ye sd ℘cinct for ye paymen[ ] of ye Sexton there being in ye sd ℘cinct this year 176 Tiths which Cums to [ ]

Credett Due to y^e ℘inct 20^lb Tob^o Ordered to pay Mr Neele 200^lb

Test Henry Bolton Cl^r vestry Kingston ℘ish

North River
℘cinct ʃʃ 1707

Ordered that Mr Peter Ransone do forthwith Collect 1^lb Tob^o ℘ pole throug[ ] ye said ℘scinct for ye satesfaction of ye Sexton there being in ye S^d Pscinct this [ ] 166 Tiths

ordered to pay Mr Th^o Neale Sexton 186^lb Tob^o

Credett due to Mr Neale 14^lb Tob^o

Test Henry Bolton Cl^{r} ves^{t} Kings ꝑish

North River
ꝑsinct 1708

Ordered that Mr William Elliott Churchwarden do Collect one pound of Tob^{o} ꝑ p[ ] Through ye S^{d} ꝑscinct for ye Satesfaction of ye Sexton there being in ye S^{d} ꝑscinct this year 169 Tiths Ordered to pay Mr Th^{o} Neale Sexton 169^{lb} Tob^{o}

Credett due to Mr Neale 45^{lb} Tob^{o}

Test Henry Bolton Cl^{r} King^{s} ꝑish

North River
ꝑscincts ſs 1709

Ordered that Mr Robert Elliott Churchwarden do Collect too pounds & hal[ ] of Tobacko ꝑ pole of Each Tithable ꝑson within ye S^{d} ꝑscincts for ye Sattesfaction of ye Sexton & other y^{e} ꝑish Credetors there being within ye S^{d} ꝑscincts y^{s} ꝑsent yeare 168 Tithables

	lb Tob^{o}
To pay Wm Smith for too Casements	200
To pay Th^{o} Neale Sexton	200
To pay Th^{o} Neale on a Reares	45
	445

Tes^{t} Henry Bolton Cl^{r} vest^{r} Kings^{t} ꝑish

(10)

[ ] Att a meeting on ye 30th of September 1710
[ ]scinct

P^{r}sent
Capt Ambros Dudley
Mr Peter Ransone
Mr Robert Elliott

Ordered That Capt Ambros Dudley Churchwarden do Collect one pound & halfe of Tobako of Each Tithable ꝑson within ye S^{d} ꝑscinct: & To pay Mary Neale Sexton Too hundred pounds of Tobako & to keepe ye Rest in his Hands tell next yeare there Being in ye Sd ℔scincts ye yeare 167 Tithables

Test Henry Bolton Clr Vestr Kingst pish

[ ]rth River ℔ at a meeting on ye 13th day of September
[ ]ct 1711

Capt Ambros Dudley
℔sent mr Robert Elliott Vestrymen
mr Peter Ransone

Ordered that Mr Peter Ransone do Collect one pound & halfe of Tobacko ℔ pole of Each Tithable ℔son with In ye Said ℔scinct & to pay William Tompkins Sexton Too hundred pounds of tobaco & to leve ye Rest In William Tompkins hands tell next yeare there being in ye Said ℔scinct this yeare 163 Tithables

Test Henry Bolton Clr Vestr Kingst ℔ish

[ ]orth River At a meeting on ye 14th day of octo-
[ ]scinct ſs ber 1712 ℔sent Capt Ambros Dudley & Mr Robert Elliott Vest Me

Ordered	lb Tob
to pay Capt Thomas Todd for a box of Leed Sawder & glaſs	300
to pay Mr Richard Jueson for mending ye Chapell windows	250
to pay Mr Tomkins for his trouble & aſsistance	100
to pay William Tomkins Sexton	200
	850

Cor Cr		
by Capt Ambros Dudley	50lb Tobo	
by Mr William Tomkins	44	
	94	94

[ ]e whole Charge being 756lb Tobo which 756

devided by 151 ye number of tithables this yeare Coms to 5lb tobo ꝑ pole Mr Robert Elliott being Churchwarden [ ]is year is ordered to Collect ye Same

Test Henry Bolton Clr Vestry Kingst ꝑish

North River ꝑscinct — Att A meeting on ye 30th day of September 1713 by ye vestry Men of ye Sd ꝑScinct

Ordered That Capt Ambros Dudley do Collect 2 pounds of Tobacko ꝑ pole of Each Tithable ꝑson within ye Sd ꝑscinct there being in ye Sd ꝑscinct this yeare 152 Tithables

	lb Tobo
To pay William Tomkins Sexton	200
Tobo due to Capt Dudley To pay Henry Bolton	118
	318

Test Henry Bolton Clr vestr Kings ꝑish

North River ꝑscinct — Att A Meeting on ye 7th day of February 17 14/15 presant Capt Ambros Dudley & Mr Robert Elliott Vesr M[ ]

Ordered that 2 pounds of Tobaco ꝑ pole be Levied Through the Sd ꝑscinct & to pay ye Same as followeth in there b[ ] in ye Sd ꝑscinct 146 Tithables

To pay William Tompkins Sexton	200
To pay Capt Ambros Dudley	14

Test Hen: Bolton Clr vesr King ꝑ[ ]

(11)

W[ ] Tom Dr	
To old acco	78
To ye payt	146
	224

At a vestry he'd ye 29th of September 1715 at ye Eastermost River Church

Ordered that One pound of Tobako ꝑ pole be Collected Through

Credet ℘ sall	200
Due to ℘cinct	24

the Nor[ ] River Prscinct & ye Same payd unto William Tompkins Sexton. There being [ ] Sd ℘scinct this present yeare 146 Tithables: Testo Henry Bolton Clr vestry Kings ℘is[ ]

Wm Tom Dtr to old acco	24
To ye years payt	157
	181
By Credt: ye years Salr	200
Due to Wm Tom	19

At a vestry held ye 2d of october 1716 for ye Parish of Kingston

Ordered that one pound of Tobako ℘ pole be Collected through ye North Ri[ ] Prscinct & the Same payd unto William Tompkins Sexton there being in ye [ ] Prscinct this present yeare 157 Tithables: Test Henry Bolton Clr vesr Kings ℘[ ]

Wm Tom Detr	312
Credt ℘ Salr	200
Cr ℘ last accot	019
	219
Wm Tom Detr to ye ℘Scinct	93

At a meeting of ye North River ℘cinct Vestry Men on ye 25th of November 1717

Ordered that two pounds of Tobako ℘ pole be Collected by Mr John Tabb Churchwar[ ] Through ye Said ℘cinct & ye Same payd unto William Tompkins Sexton there be[ ] In ye Sd ℘scinct this present year 156 Tithables; Test Henry Bolton Clr vestr Kis ℘[ ]

Wm Tom Detr to	149
To last yeare	93
	242
Credet ℘ Salr	200
Due to ye ℘scit	42

At A Meeting of ye Vestry Men of the North River ℘Scinct on ye 29th of September 17[ ]

Ordered that Mr John Tabb Church warden do Collect one pound of Tobako [ ] Pole of Each Tithable ℘son Through ye Sd ℘cinct & to pay ye Same unto William Tompkins Sexton there being in ye Sd ℘scinct this present year 149 Tithable[ ]

Test Henry Bolton
Clr vestr Kings ℘ish

Wm Tomp Detr	306
To last years acco	42
	348
Cred by Salr	200
Due to ye ℘cinct	148

At A Meeting of ye Vestry Men of ye North River ℘cinct on ye 29th of 7ber 17[ ]

Ordered that Mr Robert Elliott Churchwarden do Collect two pounds of Tobak[ ] Pole of Each Tithable ℘son through ye Sd ℘scinct & to pay ye Same unto Willia[ ] Tompkins Sexton there being in ye Sd ℘cinct this present yeare 153 Tithables

Tests Henry Bolton
Clr vestr Kings ℘[ ]

Wm Tomp Detr	154
To last years accot	148
	302
Cr ℘ Salery	200
Due to ye ℘cinct	102

At A Meeting of ye Vestry Men of ye North River ℘cinct on ye 29th of September 1720

Ordered that Mr Robert Elliott Churchwarden do Collect one pound of Tobako ℘ Pole of Each Tithable ℘son through ye Sd ℘cinct & to pay ye Same to William Tompkins Sexton there being in ye Sd ℘Scinct this ℘sent yeare 154 Tithables

Tests Henry Bolton
Clr Vestr Kingst ℘ish

Wm Tomp Dtr to	168
to last years accot	102
	270

At a Meeting of ye Vestry Men of ye North River ℘cinct on ye 3d of October 172[ ]

Ordered yt Mr George Dudley

Cr ꝑ Salery	200
Due to ye ꝑcinct	70

Church Warden do Collect one pound of Tobako [ ] Pole of Each Tithable ꝑson through ye Sd ꝑcinct & to pay ye Same to William Tompkins Sexton there being in ye Sd ꝑcinct this yeare 168 Tithables

Tests Henry Bolton
Clr vestr Kingst ꝑish

Mrs Tompkins Dtr to	173
to old accot	70
	243
Cr ꝑ Salr	200
due to ye ꝑcinct	43

At a meeting of ye Vestry Men of ye North River ꝑcinct on ye 29th of September 1722

Ordered yt Capt George Dudley Church Warden do Collect one pound of Tobacco ꝑ pole of Each tithable ꝑson throug ye Sd ꝑcinct & to pay ye Same to Mrs Sarah Tompkins Sexton there being in the Said ꝑcinct this yeare 173 Tithables

Tests Henry Bolton
Clr vest Kingst ꝑi[ ]

Mrs Tompkins Dtr to	177
To last Eares Accot	43
	220
Crt By ye years Sallery	200
Due to ye ꝑscinct	020

At a Meeting of ye Vestry Men of ye North River ꝑsinct on ye 30th: of September 1723

Ordered that Mr William Elliott Churchwarden do Collect one pound of Tobako ꝑ pole of Each tithable ꝑson through ye Sd ꝑsinct & to pay ye Same to Mrs Sarah Tompkins S[ ] There being in ye Said ꝑsinct this ꝑsent yeare 177 Tithables

Tests Henry Bolton
Clr Vestry Kingston ꝑish

(12)

[ ]pkins D^{tr}	198
[ ] Acco	20
	218
[ ] ye years	
[ ]y	200
[ ]^{e} ℘scinct	18

Att A Meeting of ye vestry Men of ye North River ℘cinct on ye 29th of September 1724

Ordered that Mr William Elliot Churchwarden do Collect one pound of Tobako ℘ pole of Each Tithable ℘son throw ye Said ℘sinct & to pay ye Same to Mrs Sarah Tompkins Sexton there Being in the Said ℘sinct this present Yeare 198 Tithables

Tes^{ts} Henry Bolton
Cl^{r} Vestry Kingst ℘ish

1725

[ ]dered by ye Gen^{t} Men of ye vestry of North River ℘sinct that one pound of Tobako ℘ pole be Collected Through The S^{d} ℘cinct & to Receve of John Tompkins 18^{lb} of Tobako & with ye Same to pay for ye Lock for ye Chapel dore And ye Sextons according to Agreement

Tes^{t} Henry Bolton Cl^{r} ves^{r} Kings ℘ish

1726

[ ]dered by ye Ge^{t} Me of ye vestry of North River ℘cinct that one pound of Tobacko ℘ pole be Collected throug[ ] The S^{d} ℘cinct & To pay ye Same To Richard Creedle Sexton. ye Number of Tithables being 204

Tes^{ts} Henry Bolton Cl^{r} Vestr Kingston ℘ish

(13)

Att a Vestry Held for Kingston Parrish the 29th day of Sep[ ]

The Gen^{t} preſent The Revd Mr Jno Blacknall, Capt George Dudley Mr Charles Debnom Gen^{t}: M^{r}: Jno Hayes Mr Jno Billups M[] Marlow Capt Thomas Hayes Mr Hugh Gwyn Capt Robert Barnard Gen^{t} of the Vestry ordered

Tobacco

To The Revd Mr Jno Blacknall	16000 and Cask
To Ditto for Quitrents	00128
To Ditt^{o} for Wine	00360
To Capt Jno Cleaton	00065
To Thomas Machen	00540
To Sarah Hunley for Elizabeth Anderton	00125
To Capt Robert Barnard for Matt Thos for a basterd Child	00900 Next year 7[ ]
To Sarah Barton	00300
To Thomas Longest for a parrish Child	00600
To Francis Lendall for oner powers	00400
To Ann Powers Sexton	00300
To Thos: Putnom Sexton	00600
To Thomas Hill for a parrish Child & to Discharge ye Parrish	00700
To Thomas Willis for to Discharge his Leve	00060
To Larance Collins	00300
To Edward Wyatt Shirreff	00060
To Thomas Bridge Daughter	00300
To Wm Brookes Cleark	01700 and Cask
	24038

It is ordird by the above Vestry that Mr Charles Blacknall Collect of Each Tithable perſon within This Said parrish 22½ pounds of Tobacco for the Uſe of the Minester Cleark and other parrish Creadet, it is furder orderd that the above Said Collectter Receive of Each Tithable perſon in the Said parrish 20 pounds of Tobacco for the Churches now in building

orderd by the above Said Vistry that the Tobacco now In Capt Barnards Hands be put In Cask

Capt Robt Barnard Mr Hugh Gwyn Churchwardins
Tithables I[ ] parrish This Year 1148
22½ per pol[ ]

Teſt Wm Brookes C:l

(14)

Att a Vestry Held for Kingston Parrish the 6th day of April 1741

Pſent The Rev[d] Jn[o] Blacknall Cap[t] George Dudley Cap[t] Tho[s] Hayes Cap[t] Robert Barnard M[r] W[m] Armistead M[r] Jn[o] Hayes M[r] Jn[o] Billups M[r] Hugh Gwyn M[r] Charles Debnam

It was agreed on by the Said Gen[t]: of the Vestry That M[r] Moore and M[r] W[m] Rand do Take all The New Brick wall Down which They put Up and Build y[e] Said wall up againe, with good Brickes & good Morter Workmanlike and to do it with all Experdition So that The whole Building is to be well performed By the Last Day of July Next

and The Said More and Rand to Repare all Damages the old Church hath Sustained by Them, and it is further agreed that M[r] Rand Rep[r] what is wanting to The old Church and to make a pew Each Side the Commuon Table and To bring his Acc[t] to the Next Vestry, it further Agread That Thom[s]: Dawſon Serve as Cleark at The New Church Till Whitsontide Upon Liking and if approve[d] on to Continue for one Thousand pounds of Tobacco p[r] Yeare Cap[t] Robert Barnard to Take Bond and Security of the above More and Rand

Test W[m] Brookes C: V: K

1741 order of payments to be Made Next Year as followes Viſt

	Tobacco
To Thomas Michen for Tho[s] Putnom & wife	1000
To Tho[s] Daves for a Basterd Child	0500
To W[m] Brable for a basterd Child	0500
To Mary Magerſon	0300
To Robert Reves	0600
To W[m] Maſon	0500
To Thomas Capril	0300
To Thomas Longest	0400
	4100

It is further agreed by the said gen[t] to Leve Ten pounds

of Tobacco p^{r} Pole for the Church now in Reparing

Teſt Wm Brookes

15)

Att a Vestry Hild for Kingston parrish the 29th day of Octob[ ] 1741

The Gen^{t} of The Vistry preſent The Revd Mr Jno Blacknall Co^{lo} Henry Armistead Capt Robt Barnard M^{r} Jno: Billup[ ] Mr Hugh Gwyn Capt Thomas Hayes Mr Jno Hayes Capt George Dudley Mr Charles Debnom Mr Wm Marlow

It was order^{d} by the Said Vestry *That *M^{r}

	Tobacco
To ye Revd Mr Jno Blacknall	16000 & Cask
To Ditt^{o} for Quitrents of The Gleabe land	00128
To Ditt^{o} for wine for the Church	00360
To Sarah Burton	00400
To Francis Lendall for oner Powers	00400
To Elizabeth Turner	00300
To Geo: Elliott for Thomas putnom & wife	01000
To Matt. Thomas for a basterd Child	00700
To Ann Pallester Sexton	00300
To Ava^{r}: Cantrell Sexton	00067
To Caleb Hunley for Ann power Sexton	00233
To Thomas Peak and Thomas Bridge	00300
To Thomas Dawſon Cleark	00500
To Larance Collins	00300
To Capt Jno Cleaton	00255
To James Wyatt Sheriff	00080
To Wm Brookes Cleark	01700 & Cask
To Wm Brookes for Taring the Churches	01300
	24323 Depose^{r}
To 8 per C^{t}: on 18188 is	01455 211
To 4 p^{r} C^{t}: on 06135 is	00246
24323	26024 by 1166 Tithables is 22½ p^{r} Po[ ]

* These two words scratched through in the MS.—C. G. C.

It was orderd that Mr Charles Blacknall be Collectr for ye above Sd Yeare

Collo Henry Armistead and Mr Charles Debnam be Churc[ ] wardins for ye said yeare

It Is further agreed on by the Said Gent of ye Vistry, that Mr William Rand is to Repare all the Body of The old Cha[ ] and to Make New window frames, and Sashes, and to fill the said windowes With good Crown glaſs, and to ha[ ] all the old glaſs and other Stuff To his one Uſe and at the Trew performance of the Said work to Rece fifty [ ]nds Curant Cash for so doing

[ ]

(16)

Acct of What is ordred to be paid Next year 1743

	Ttobacco
To Richard Marchant for Thos: Putnam	600
To Robert Reves for Keeping ye Same Child	500
[ ]o Thos Daves	400
[ ] Wm Brable	400
[ ]o Anna Hudgen for Keeping ye Same Chd	700
	2600

Capt Geo. Dudley

To pay Francis Lendall 10s/ and Richd Davis 2/6

Mr Wm Armistead and Capt Ambroſs Dudley Churchwardins for the year 1743

Capt Ambroſs Dudley Collectter

Teſt Wm Brookes Cl: V.

(17)

Att A Vestry held for Kingston Parrish at ye New Church the 4th day of October 1742

Gent of the Vestry preſent The Rivd Mr Jno Blacknall Capt Geo: Dudley Mr Wm Elliott Mr John Hayes Mr John Billups Mr Hugh Gwyn Mr Wm Armistead Capt Ambroſs Dudley

ordered	Tobacco
To the Rev[d]: M[r] Jn[o] Blacknall	16000 & Cask
To Di[tto] f Quitrents of y[e] Gleabe Land	00128
To Ditt[o] for Wine for y[e] Church	00360
To Ditt[o] for two Surples	01550
To Cap[t] Jn[o] Cleaton	00140
To Averilah Cantrill Sexton	00400
To Thomas Davis for a basterd Child	00500
To W[m] Brable for a basterd Child	00500
To Robert Reves for a parrish Child	00600
To W[m] Mason for a basterd Child	00500
To Thomas Longest for a basterd Child	00400
To Henry putnam for Mary Magerſon	00300
To Sarah Burton	00500
To Thomas Caprill	00389
To Thomas Dawſon	01100 & Cask
To W[m] Marchant for W[m] Putnam	00050
To Elizabeth Turner	00300
To Ann Palester Sexton	00300
To Thomas Bridge for his Lame Daughter	00300
To Elizabeth Longeſt for James Longest	00800
To Doc[t] Roche acc[t] for James Longest	01434
To Thomas Mahen for Thomas Putnam	00800
To Francis Lendall for Powers Daughter	00400 Dep[r] 103
To Ann Hudgen for Keeping James Longests Child	00500
To Larance Collins	00300
To W[m] Brookes Cleark	01700 & Cask
To James Cray for one Leve over Charged	00032½
To Richard Daves one Leve over Charge	00032½
To Robert fliping over Charged	00032½
	[ ]

(18)

Att a Vestry Hild for Kingstone Parrish the 12th Day of october 1743

Gen[t] preſent The Rev[d] M[r] Blacknall Mineſter Cap[t] George

Dudley Mr. William Armiſtead Gent: Mr John Hayes Mr William Marlow Mr John Billups Mr Hugh Gwyn Capt Thomas Hayes

Orderd	Tobacco
To the Reverand Mr Blacknall Minester	16000 and Cask
To Ditto for quitrents	00128
To Ditto for Wine	00360
To James Wyatt	00027
To Capt John Cleaton	00018
To Robert Reves for a parrish Child	00500
To Thomas Daves for a Basterd Child	00400
To William Brable for a Basterd Child	00400
To Ann Hudgen for James Longest Child	00700
To Mrs: Ann Armistead for Thomas Putnam	00600
To Sarah Burton	00500
To Francis Lendall for James Powers Daughter	00400
To Richard Hodges for one Leve over paid	00028
To Charles Hunley for one Leve over paid	00028
To Thomas Capril for his wife	00300
To Mary Bolton for William Putnam	00150
To Ellonor Huts	00200
To Thomas Bridge for his Lame Daughter	00300
To Elizabeth Turner	00400
To Larance Collins	00300
To Wm Young	00400
To Thomas Willis	00500
To Richard Longest for a parrish Child	00450
To Honnor Whimpy	00126
To Thomas Hunley for Roſe Michell	00350
To Ann Pallister Sexton	00300
To Widdow Cantrill Sexton	00300
To Thomas Dawſon Cleark	01100 and Cask
To Doctr: Symmer	01794
To Caleb Hunley for Clearing ye Church yeard	00200
To James McCollet	00163

To William Brookes Cleark Church & Vistry	01700 and Cask
	29122
10 pr Ct on 19288 is	1928
6 pr Ct on 9834	591
	31641

Capt Gwyn Reade Capt Kemp Plumer Chose Vestrymen
Mr Wm Marlow Collectr and Churchwardin
Capt Kemp Plumer Churchward
orderd for Thomas Hunley for Rose Michell Next year 500
To Easter Bohanon for Thomas Putnam Next year 300
Leve 27 pr pole Tithables 1176
Test Wm Brookes Cleark

(19)
Att a Vestry Hild for Kingston Parrish ye first day of [ ]
Gent. Men prsent the Revd John Blacknall Capt George Dudley Capt Ambross Dudley Mr John Hayes Mr John Billup[ ] Capt Robert Barnard Mr William Marlow Vestrym[ ]

	Tobacco
To ye Revd John Blacknall	16488 and Cask
To John Blacke for a parish Child	00700
To John Matthes	00044
To Robert Reves	00300
To Sarah Burton	00300
To Elliner Dewplisey	00300
To Ann Palliser	00300
To Thomas Jarrott for Sarah welch	00108
To Elizabeth Turner	00200

	To Marcus Bendickson	00200	
	To Thomas Bridge's Daughter	00300	
	To Thomas Putnom Sexton	00250	
	To Thomas Hill for a parish Child	00700	
	To Thomas Longest for parish Child	00700	Next Year 600
	To Capt John Cleaton	00125	
	To Edward Wyatt	00170	
	To Larance Collins	00400	
[ ]16 Tithables	To Sarah Hunley	00150	
26 & 25 Leves	To James powers Sexton	00300	
	To Caleb Hunley	00100	
	To Doctr John Symer	03069	
	To Henry Putnom	00200	
	To William Brookes Clark C: V	01768	and Cask
	To 18256 @ 8 pr Ct is	01460	2
	To 4 pr Ct on 8919 is	00356	9
		28998	

Orderd That Capt Robert Barnard Receive of Each Tithable Perʃon Within ye above Said parish 26 pounds of Tobac[ ] for the Use of the minester and other parish Creadit The Said Barnard is orderd to Receive of Each of the above Said Tithables 25 pounds of Tobacco for the use of the New Church Furniture and Reparing the old Church

[ ]he Said Gentmen Hath further agreed with Mr. Jno: more & Mr Wm. Rand to ad a bulding to ye North Side of the Eastermoʃt Church of 25 foot Each way with a brick wall of the Same Thickneʃs of ye old wall with a gallirey and Three windos and a dore at the Eand and to shingle the Said Side of the

Church with g[ ] Shingles Laid on workman Like and to have and Receive for so doing 200^{lb} Curant Cash

Wm Brooke [ ]

(20) [Blank in MS.—C. G. C.]

(21)

Att Vestry Hild for Kingston Parrish ye 30th day of October 1744

Gen^{t} of the Vestry p^{r}eſent the Revd Mr John Blacknall Capt George Dudley Mr Charles Debnam Mr William Elliott Mr John Billups Mr William Marlow Capt Gwyn Reade Capt Thomas Hayes Capt Kemp Plumer

	Tobacco
To ye Revd John Blacknall	16000 and Cask
To Ditt^{o} for quitrents	00128
To Ditt^{o} for Wine for the Church	00360
To Capt John Cleaton	00060
To Thomas Hunley for Roſe Michell 2 monthes 500 p^{r} Yeare	83½
To Sarah Edwards for Roſe Michell 10 months @ 500	00416½
To Francis Armiſtead for Thomas Putnam	00300
To Thomas Machen for [*] Bridges	00015
To Ann Lendal for Powers Daughter	00400
To Richard Hunley for one Leve over paid Last year	00027
To Thomas Peake for Ditt^{o}	00027
To John Forreſt Junr for Ditto for two Leves over paid	00054
To James Harper for Ditt^{o}	00027
To Ann Collins	00300
To Thomas Bridge for his Daughter	00300
To Elizabeth Turner	00400
To Mary Creadle	00300
To Thomas Willis	00500

* This word is illegible. Probably it should be read Francis.—C. G. C.

To Charles Baker for buring Caprils Wife	00200	
To Capt Pumer for Caprils Wife	00300	
To Ellener Hutts	00200	
To Elizabeth Cleark for Sarah Burton	00500	
To Joyce Dewplicey	00200	
To Mary Parrott for a parrish Child	00250	
To Thomas Longeſt for a parrish Child	00400	
To Thomas Dawſon Cleark	01100	and Cask
To Richard Longeſt for a parrish Child	00600	
To Ann Pallister Sexton	00300	
To Widow Cantril Sexton	00300	
To George Elliott for Billins Sadler	00600	
To Robert Reves for a parrish Child and to Bare the parish Harmles from the said Child but not to have his Tobacco till he hath Given the parish Bond and Security	00500	
To Mr William Marlow for three Leves @ 27 pr Pole	00081	
To William Brookes Cleark of C: and Vestry	01700	and Cask
	26929	
Capt Kemp Plumer Collicter Capt Kemp Plumer and Mr William Marlowe Churchwardins for this prſent Year		Tithables 1170
10 10 pr Ct on 19288 is	1928	Leve 25½
To 6 pr Ct on 7641 is	0458	
	29315	

ordered to Sarah Edwards Next year for Roſe Michell 500lb Tobacco

orderd that William Brookes Cleark shall have the Deposeter yearly

Teſt William Brookes C[ ]

(22)

Att A Vestry Hild for Kingston Parrish the 7th day of October 1745

Gent present the Revd Mr John Blacknall Capt Geo: Dudley Mr John Hayes Mr Charles Debnam Mr Wm Marlow Mr John Billups Capt Ambross Dudley Mr Hugh Gwyn Capt Thomas Hayes Capt Gwyn Reade Capt Kemp Plumer

Ordered	Tobacco	
To the Revd Mr John Blacknall	16000	& Cask
To Ditto for quitrents of the Gleabe Land	00128	
To Ditto for Wine	00360	
To Capt John Cleaton for the List of Tithables	00020	
To Ann Pallester Sexton	00300	
To Sarah Edwards for Keeping Rose Michell	00500	
To Ann Lendall for Keeping oner powers	00400	
To Richard Longest for Keeping a parrish Child	00500	
To Thomas Willis	00500	
To Ellener Hutts	00200	
To Averila Bridge	00300	
To Mary Creadle	00300	
To Elizabeth Turner	00400	
To Margreat Neithcut	00400	
To Averila Cantrell Sexton	00300	
To Capt Kemp Plumer for 4 Leves Runaway out ye Parrish	00101	
To Thomas Dawson Cleark	01100	& Cask
To Doct John Symmer for good Bought of James McCollot for James Cleark and Rebecca Jonson	00656	
To Doct Symmer for Bording James Cleark and Rebecca Jonson and the Curing of the Sd James' Clearkes Legg, and Curing and Keeping the Said Rebecca Jonson Cleare from all Charges that may hapen for Two years from this Date	05800	Tithables 1196 @ 27¾ per Pole

To Robert parrott	00500
To Wm Brookes Cleark	01700 & Cask
	30465 Depr 125

To 10 pt: on 19288 is 1928¾
To 6 pert on 11177 is 670¾

30465

To Francis Singleton Widdow £ 4: 0s: 0d Cash to be paid by Capt Plumer out of a fine In his one hands and one In Joſeph Davis hands, and the Said Capt plumer is to pay to Mr William Tabb 12/6 out of the above Said fines for five Bushalls of wheat The Said Capt Kemp Plumer Is appointed Collecter for this preſent Year 1745

ordered By the Said gent men the Churchwardins for this parrish do meet at the gleabe houſe of this parrish at any time appointted to agree with workmen to Repare the Said gleabe houſe Mr John Hayes and Capt Gwyn Reade is appointed Church wardines for this preſen year

Teſt Wm Brookes C V K

(23)

Att A Vestry held for Kingston parish the 13th day of October 1746

Gent present the Revd Mr Blacknall Capt George Dudley Mr William Elliott Mr John Billups Mr John Hayes Mr Charles Debnam Mr Hugh Gwyn Capt Thos Hayes Mr William Marlow Mr William Armistead Capt Gwyn Reade Capt Kemp Plumer

Orderd

To the Revd Mr Blacknall	16000 & Cask
To Ditto for wine	00360
To Ditto for quitrents	00128
To Capt John Clayton	00085
To Ann Palister Sexton	00300
To Roſe Mitchel	00500

To Onner Powers	00400
To Thos Willis	00500
To Robt Spencer for a parish Child	00500
To Ellener Huts	00300
To Avereler Bridge	00300
To Mary Creedle	00400
To Elizabeth Turner	00400
To Averela Cantril	00300
To Thomas Dawſon	01100 & Cask
To Doc^{t} John Symer for Robt Parrott	00690
Francis Singleton	00500
To the Revd Mr Blacknall for Plastring the gleebe house	00534
To Lucy Sumers	00200
To Capt Plumer for three levies gon Out the County	00082¼
To Abr: Marchant for keeping of Johnsons Child till crismus	00300
To 10 p^{r} C^{t} on 19288 is	01928¾
To 6 p^{r} C^{t} on 6291 is	00377
To William Brookes Cleark	01700 & Cask
	27885

To Richard Davis in cash 3/6
To Capt Plumer to pay Thos Dawſon for a dyal & post 7/6 — 1251 Titha^{bl}
Mr Charles Blacknall to pay Sans Smith £5 ‖ 17^{s} ‖ 10^{d} For Work don to the Gleebe house To Richd Hunley 15/ — Dep^{r}: 262
Capt George Dudley p^{d} the Ballance of his Acc^{t} for Shingles to Mr Charles Blacknall £ 1‖8^{s}‖6^{d}
Mr William Armistead Colec^{t}
Mr William Armistead Major Ambroſe Dudley

(24)
Att a Vestry Hild for Kingston Parrish ye 26th. day of October 1747

The Vistry Men preſent The Revd: Mr John Blacknall Capt: George Dudley Mr John Hayes Mr John Billups Capt Kemp Plumer Majr Ambroſ Dudley Capt Thomas Hayes

orderd:	Tobacc
To the Revd Mr John Blacknall	16000 and Cask
To Ditto for wine for the Church	00360
To Ditto for quitrents for the gleabe Land	00128
To Capt John Cleaton	00197
To Thomas Machen	00077
To Mr James Hill for Taking Joyce a Child of Thos Plises of The Parrish	00300
Mr John Hayes to pay Mr Thomas Booth 14/4	
Mr John Hayes to pay Thomas Dawſon 5/	
To Ann Collins for Keeping Thomas plises Child	00450
To Abroham Rice for Keeping a nother of plises Children	00450
To John Buſh for Keeping of Plises Children	00050
To Ann Collins and Abroham Rice for Keeping two of Thomas Pises Children next Yeare 500lb Tobacco for Each Child	
To Abroham Marchant for Jonſons Child	00400
To Francis Singleton Widdo	00800
To the widdo Cantrill for Keeping Jane Hunley & Sexton	01100
Mr John Hayes to pay Wil-	

liam Brookes Junr: 15/8
Major Ambroſs Dudley to pay
to Wm Brookes Junr 4/4
To Capt Thomas Hayes for
Keeping oner powers 00600
To Elloner Hutts 00300
To Ann Pallester 00300
To Thomas Willies 00500
To Averilia Bridge 00300
To Thomas Dawſon Cleark 01200 and Cask
To Roſe Michell 00500 1287
To Mary Creadle 00400 Tithables
To Elizabeth Turner 00400 at 23lb pr Pole
To Lucy Sumers 00200 Depoeter 91
To Margret Nithercut 00400
To William Brookes for Vetry
and Church 01700 and Cask
Majr Ambroſs Dudley to ye
Revd: Mr Blacknall 20/ 27112 Mr Charles Debnom
10 pr Ct of 19288 is 1928¾ and Mr John Billups
6 pr Ct on 7822 is 0469¼ Churchwardins

29510

(25)

Att A Vestry Hild for Kingston Parrish the 20th day of October 1748

Gent Men preſt Capt George Dudley Mr: William Armistead Mr William Elliott Mr John Billups Mr William Marlow Mr John Hayes Mr Hugh Gwyn Capt Kemp Plumer

To Mrs: Ann Blacknall 8141½ And Cask
To Capt John Cleaton 0234
To Thomas Machen 0054
To Doct John Symer 1:9:9 @ 14 pert: 0212
To Mr Robert Billups 0500
To Mr Robert Reade 0500
To Mr: John Billups 0060

To Richard Hunley Junr for Rackes	0120	
To Ann Palister	0300	
To Ann Collins for a parrish Child	0500	
To Abraham Marchant for Johnſons Child	0400	
To Abraham Rice for Do:	0500	
To George Hudgons for Jane hunley To be paid by wilkinson Hunley for ten months @ 800lb of Tobaco pr year or In money 14 pr Ct		
To Oner Powers	0600	
To Elener Hutts	0500	
To Averilah Bridge	0300	
To Thomas Dawſon Cleark	1200	And Cask
To Roſe Michall	0500	
To Mary Creedle	0400	
To Elizabeth Beard	0300	
To Lucy Sumers	0300	
To Margret Neithcut	0400	
To Con Sadler	0400	
To John Hudgen	0200	
To Thomas Caprill	0600	
To Averileah Contrill Sexton	0300	
To William Brookes	1700	and Cask
	19221	1303 Tithables
To 10 pr Ct on 11041 is	1104	Deposeter 33
To 6 pr Ct on 8180 is	490	Leve 16 pr pole
19221	20815	

Mr Wm Elliott Elliott Collectr.

Mr Wm: Elliott and Mr Hugh Gwyn Churchwardins this year

Teſt Wm Brookes C

(26)

Att A Vestry Hild for Kingston Parrish ye 10th day of October 1749

Gent. of the Vestry Preſent Capt George Dudley Mr. William Marlow Mr John Hayes Capt Thos: Hayes Mr John Billups Mr William Elliott Mr Charles Debnom Mr Hugh Gwyn Capt Gwyn Majo Ambroſs Dudley

To The Revd Mr John Dickson	3113 And Cask
To Thos Dawſon Cleark	1200 And Cask
To Ann Palister	0300
To Capt John Cleaton	0076½
To Thomas Machen	0027
To Thomas Dawſon	0150
To Joſeph Davis	0114
To Avarila Bridge to be paid to Anthony Degge Junr:	0300
To Avarila Cantrell Sexton	0300
To Mr William Marlow for a Child of Thos Plises And to Keepe the parrish Harmleſs after	0500
To Aroham Rice for Keeping a parrish Child	0300
To Capt Thomas Hayes of oner Powers	1000
To Elliner Hutts	0500
To Roſe Michall	0500
To Lucy Sumers	0300
To Margrett Neithercut	0400
To John Hudgen for a parrish Child Keept from the 23d day of Sepr att 750lb pr year	
To Lanley Billups for a parish Child And to Keep the Parrish Harnleſs	0500
To William Brable for a parrish Child Wm Brable to have Next year 750	0600
To Mary Longeſt	0370
To Capt Thos Hayes	0075
To Ann Lendall	0500
To William Brookes CC & Vestry	1700 and Cask
	12825½

10 p^{r} C^{t} on 6013 is	601¼	1340 Tithables
6 p^{r} C^{t} on 6812 is	408¾	Deposeter 236
13834½	13835½	

Cap[t] Thomas Hayes And M[r] William Marlow is Church-wardins
M[r]: William Marlow Collect[r]
The Gen[t] of the Vistrey agread to Leve 3[lb] of Tobacco per pole

Teſt William Brookes CC

(27)
At a Vestry Hild at the Parrish of Kingston in the County of Glocester y[e] 24th of october 1749

Preſent

Thomas Hayes
William Marlow
Churchwardins
George Dudley
John Hayes
Charles Debnom
William Elliott
Ambroſs Dudley

It was agreed that y[e] Reve[d] M[r] Richard Locke Should be Rec[d] as minester of the afore Said Parrish

Teſt William Brookes C V

Att a Vestry hild for Kingston Parrish the 26[th] day of June 1750

Gen[t]men preſent The Rever[d]: M[r] Richard Locke Minester Cap[t] George Dudley M[r] W[m] Armistead M[r]. W[m] Marlow M[r] W[m] Ellio[ ] Cap[t] Tho[s]. Hayes M[r] John Hayes M[r] Charles Debnom Cap[t] Gwyn Reade M[r] Hugh Gwyn

It Was Orderd by the ABove Said Gen[t]. that Robert Reade do Truley Repare the Gleabe houſe not Disturbing the Rev[d] M[r] Locke No more then he Cant Covenantley help

Teſt W[m] Brookes C V

(28)

Att Vestry Hild for Kingstone Parrish y[e] firſt day of October 1750

Preſent The Rev[d] Richard Lock Minester

Cap[t] Geo: Dudley M[r]: William Armistead Cap[t] Tho[s] Hayes M[r] John Billups Cap[t] Gwyn Reade Cap[t] Kemp Plumer M[r] John Hayes

To the Riv[d] M[r] Lock Minester for his Ballance	9956 and Cask
To Cap[t] John Cleaton	0018
To Thomas Dawſon Cleark	1200 and Cask
To Ann Pallester Sexton	0400
To William Brable for Keeping a parish Child	0750
To John Hudgen for Keeping A parrish Child	0750
To M[r] Charles Blacknall By Acc[t] And Quitrents	0977
To Geo: Hudges for Jane Hunley Last years Ballance	0348
To Richard Hunley Jun[r]	0060
To John Tompkins for Keeping a parrish Child	0200
To Sarah Hunley for Keeping Roſe Michall	0500
To Cap[t] Thomas Hayes for Oner Powers	1000
To Cap[t] Tho[s] Hayes for Last yers arears	0125
To Joſeph King for work don to y[e] Church Lock	0033½
To Doc[r] Peter Whiting for Matthew Thomas	0717
To Lucy Somers	0300
To Charles Backer for Jane Hunley	0800
To Averilea Bridge	0300

To Abroham Rice for a parrish Child	0300	
To Elliner Hutts	0500	
To Margret Neithercut	0400	
To William Brookes	1700 and Cask	
To Ann Lendal	0500	
To John Gordin Sexton	0400	
To Mary Longest	0300	
To Markuss Deyonger	0200	
To Elexander King for Keeping a parrish Child	1000	1364 Tithables
To Joſeph Sowell for Wine	0223½	19¼ per pole
To the Revd Mr Lock	0033½	Deper 142½
To William parkes Estate for a Booke	0167	
To 10 pr Cent on 12856 is	1285½	
To 6 pr ſent on 11297 is	677¾	
	26115½	

Mr William Armistead And Capt Thomas Hayes Church-wardins

Capt Thomas Hayes Collectr:

Teſt Wm Brookes Clea: Veſtry

(29)

At A Veſtry Hild for Kingston pariſh the 10th of Decembr 1750

Present

Mr William armistead
Mr John Billups
Capt George Dudley
Mr John Hayes
Mr William Elliott
Capt Gwyn Read
Mr Charles Debnam
Capt Kemp Plummer
Mr Wm Tabb

The Rev'd Mr John Dixon is Rec'd as Miniſter of Kingſton pariſh And his Time to go on from the 25th of Octobr Laſt

Order'd That the Rev'd Mr John Dixon have power to Employ Workmen To fit up the out Houſes at the Glebe and to build A Stable 16 x 20 plank'd above and the Charge to be ſubmitted to the Veſtry

Order'd that John Davis Shall Serve as Clerk of the old Church in Kingſton Pariſh from the Laying the Pariſh Levy the firſt Day of Octob^{r} Laſt

Order'd that John Davis Recieve the Veſtry Book of Mr Wm Brooks

Sin'd John Dixon Junr Minist[ ]

At a Vestry held for Kingston Parish this 8th Day of April 1751

Gen^{t} pre^{t} The Rev'd Mr John Dixon Mr William Armistead Capt George Dudly Mr John Billups Mr John Hayes Capt Gwyn Read Mr Wm Tabb

Order'd that the Church Wardens have power to agree with workmen to make a thorough Repair of the Dwelling hous at the Glebe and to add Such Conveniencies as they Shall think Neceſsary there and on the plantation

Ordered that John Davis Shall demand and Recieve all Books and other papers Relating to the pariſh affairs Now in poſseſsion of Wm Brooks Late Clerk of the Veſtry

Order'd that Mr William Armistead Do Send to England for Church ornam^{ts} Books &c. to the Value of fifty Pounds Sterling

Sin'd John Dixon Junr Minſt[ ]

(30)

At a Veſtry held for Kingston ꝑish the 13th of May 1751

Preſent The Rev'd Mr John Dixon Cleg^{m}.

Mr Wm Armistead Mr John Hayes
Capt Georg Dudley Capt Gwyn Read
Mr John Billups Capt Kemp Plummer Gen^{t}men of y^{e} Veſtry
Mr Hugh Gwyn Mr Wm Tabb

Order'd that Mr William Armiſtead Gen^{t} Chu^{h} War^{d} be impowr'd To take up fifty Pounds Curr^{t} money on Iterest and apply the Same to purchaſe Corn to be Diſtributed among the

At a Vestry held for Kingston Parish the 13th of May 1731
Present The Revd Mr John Dixon Clerk

Mr Wm Armistead Mr John Hayes
Capt George Dudley Capt Gwyn Read } Gent men of ye Vestry
Mr John Billups Capt Kemp Plummer
Mr Hugh Gwyn Mr Wm Tabb

Ordered that Mr William Armistead Senr Chur. War. be impowr'd To take up fifty Pounds Currt money on Interest and apply the Same to purchase Corn to be Distributed among the poor of this Parish at the Discretion of the Church Wardens John Dixon Junr minister

---

Kingstone Parish } At a Vestry held for this Parish this 12 of Aug 173[illegible]
The Revered mr John Dixon Clerk

Church wardens } Mr William Armistead mr John Hayes
Capt Thomas Hayes mr John Billups } Vestry men Present
mr George Dudley Mr Chas Debnam
mr Gwyn Read mr Wm Elliott

Ordered that mr Robt Read be allowd

for A kitchen	£ 13 .. 0 .. 0
A Garden 400 foot at 3d	5 .. 0 .. 0
To a Little house	2 .. 0 .. 0
To boards & Shingles	0 .. 10 .. 0
To 34 pains of Glass at 5d	[illegible] .. 5 .. 6
for Glazing putty &c. / To 34 pains glass at 5d	0 .. 11 .. 4
for going to york	0 .. 12 .. 6
To White washing	0 .. 17 .. 3
To mending the Church Lock & hinges	6 .. 0
	£ 24 .. 7 .. 7

John Dixon Junr Minister

PAGE 30 OF THE MANUSCRIPT

poor of this Piſh at the Diſcretion of the Church Wardens
John Dixon Junr Miniſter

Kingstone Pariſh ſs At a Veſtry held for this Piſh this 14th of Augt 1751
The Rever'd mr John Dixon Clergm.

Church Wardens	Mr William Armistead	Mr John Hayes
	Capt Thomas Hayes	Mr John Billups
	Mr George Dudley	Mr Chas Debnam
	Mr Gwyn Read	Mr Wm Elliott

Vestry men Preſent

Ordered that Mr Robt Read be allow'd for A Kitchen	£13‖ 0‖0
A Garden 400 foot @ /3d	5‖ 0‖0
To a Little houſe	2‖ 5‖0
To boards & Shigles	0‖10‖0
To 34 Pains of Glaſſ @ /9d for Glazing puttey &c	1‖ 5‖6
To 34 pains glaſs @ /4d	0‖11‖4
for going to York	0‖12‖6
To White waſhing	0‖17‖3
To mending the Church Lock & hinges	6‖0
	£24‖ 7‖7

John Dixon Junr. Miniſter

(31)
Kingstone Pariſh ſs At a Veſtry held for this Pish Octobr. 7th 1751

Gentm of the Veſtry psent

The Reve'd Mr John Dixon Min:	Capt George Dudly
Capt Thomas Hayes	Capt Gwyn Read
Mr John Hayes	Mr Hugh Gwyn
Mr John Billups	Mr William Tabb

Order'd
To the Rever'd Mr John Dixon Min 1600 & Cask . . 640

To D° for wine	00450		
To D° for quitrents	00128		
To Capt John Clayton	00090		
To Mr Thomas Boswell	00063		
To the Eſtate of mr Wm Marlow Dec'd	00218		
To Thomas Dawson Clerk	01200	& cask	48
To Samuel Tompkins	00019¼		
To Charles Blacknall for Richard Brooks	00800		
To John Davis Clerk	01700	& caſk	68
To Ann pallister Sexton	00400		——
To John Gordin Sexton	00400		756
To Lucy Summars	00300		
To Ann Pallister for keeping two Orphan Children	00600		
To Wm brable for keeping a piſh Child & Due to Capt Hayes	00248		
To John Hudgen for Keeping a piſh Child	00750		
To Elisabeth Longeſt for keeping a piſh Child	00400		
To Charles Baker for keeping Jane Hunley	00800		
To Sarah Hunley for keeping Rose Michel	00500		
To Capt Thomas Hayes for keeping Oner powers	01000	1354 Tithables	
To Averillo Bridge	00300		
To Ellener Huts	00500	Deposr 33	
To Ann Lendal	00500		
To Richard Hunley for keeping Judah Cray	00500		
To John Bridg	00200		
To Eliſabeth Evans widdow & four Children	01200		
To be left in the Church wardens hands to be Sold To Discharge a bond of fifty pounds Currancy on Interst	08400		

To be left in the Church ward^{ns} hands hands to be Sold to pay the Ballance of John Peters's acc^{t} £63‖4‖4	10114	
to be left in the Church ward^{ns} hands to be Sold to pay John Peters £56‖15 for building the out houses on the glebe	09080	
	03411	Col^{rs} part
To 4 P^{r} C^{t} on 18900 allow'd for Cask Comes to	00756	
	61027	

(32)

Order'd that the twelve pound nineteen Shillings and Seven pence in Mr William Armisteads hands be paid To John peters on Demand

Mr William Armistead & Capt. Thomas Hayes appointed Church wardens for the year Ensueing

Order'd that Cap't Thomas Hayes Do Stand Col^{r} and that the S^{d} Capt Thomas Hayes Do Recieve of Each Tithable person within this S^{d} piſh 45¼ pounds of good tobacco To Satisfie the Several Creditors there is this year 1354 tithables in this pariſh

At a Vestry held for Kingston parrish the 10th of Augt. 1752

Gent^{m}	Capt Thomas Hayes	
Present	Mr John Billups	Mr Hugh Gwyn
	Mr John Hayes	Capt Kemp Plummer
	Capt Gwyn Read	Mr William Tabb

Ordered that William Brownley the son of William Brounley be levy free

Ordered that Mr John Tompkins Junr do make a thorough repair of the Old Church and bring his Charge to the Vestry for laying our Next parish levy

(33)
At a Veſtry Held for Kingston parish Octo[r] 16th 1752

The rever'd M[r] John Dixon Minister

Present		
	M[r] William Armistead	M[r] John Billups
	Cap[t] Thomas Hayes	Cap[t] Gwyn Read
	M[r] John Hayes	Cap[t] Kemp Plummer

Gent[m] Veſtry

Ordered that acct wth Cap[t] Tho[s] Hayes be Setl[d] & y[e] Ballance be p[d] to the ℘iſh from him		26‖14‖3
Order'd	lb Tobacco	
to the rever'd M[r] Dixon	16000 & Cask	
To D[o] 4 p[r] C[t] allow'd by Law	640	
To Do. 4 p[r] C[t] Not levied last year	640	
To D[o].. for quitrents	128	
Cap[t] Thomas Hayes to pay y[e] rever'd M[r] Dixon's acc[t] £13‖2		
To Thomas Dawson Clerk	1200 & Cask	
To John Davis	1700 & Cask	
To Ann Palister Sexton	400	
To Mary Gordin Sexton	400	
To Cap[t] John Clayton	67½	
That Cap[t] Tho[s] Hayes Do pay M[r] Cha[s] Blacknals acc[t]. £3‖0‖4¼		
That Cap[t] Hayes do pay Rob[t] Hunleys acct 1‖5		
To Richard Hunley for Judith Cray	300	
To Mary Gordin for Keeping a Child of Griffins	75	
To Rob[t] Jervis for Keeping a Child for D.[o].	100	1215 Tithables
To Miſs Elisabeth Green for a levy overpaid	45¼	
To M[r] Richard bentley for a levy overpaid	45¼	
To John Hugen for keeping a ℘ish		

Child & Richd Brooks	700	
To the widdow Evans & four Children	1200	
To Capt Hayes for Seven piſh levies overpaid	316¾	
To Ann Palister for keeping two Children	600	
To Elisabeth Baker for Keeping Jane Hunley	400	Total 30557¾
To George Hudgen for Keeping Averillo Bridg 4 monts	100	6 pr Ct is 1833
To Averillo Bridg	200	4 pr Ct
To Elenor Hutts	500	for cask 756
To John Bridg	200	———
To Lucy Summers	300	33146
To Roſe Michel	500	28 pr. Pole
To Ann Lendal	500	874 Deposr
To Capt Thos Hayes for Keeping oner Powers	1000	
To John Davis for keeping a ℘iſh Child	700	
To Mary Longeſt	300	
To Chriſtian Owen	300	
To Elisabeth Bridg widdow	300	
To Sarah Worden for keeping Frans. Bridges	400	
To Elisabeth Dawson for keeping Chriſn owen	300	
	30557¾	

(34)

Orderd that Sarah Baſsets Negroe woman be levy free

Capt Thomas Hayes to pay the widow McMekins £3||5s

Orderd that Capt Kemp Plummer & Mr William Tabb Do stand Church wardens for the year Ensueing

That Capt Kemp Plumer Do receive 28 pounds of tobacco of Each Tithable person in this ℘ish to Satisfie the Several Creditors

Sign'd by
the rever'd Mr John Dixon Minisr

Kingstone Parrish ſs

At a Veſtry held for this pariſh Octor 22 1753

Preſent The Reverend Mr John Dixon Minister Capt Kemp Plummer Mr William Tabb, Chuh wardens Capt George Dudley Capt Gwyn Reade Mr John Billups Mr John Hayes Capt Thomas Hayes M Charles Debnam

Ordered that tobacco be levied as follows

For the rever'd Mr John Dixon		16000 & cask
For Do for Shrinkage 4 pr Ct		00640
Do for Quitrents		128
For Thomas Dawson Clerk		1200 & cask
For John Davis Do & Clerk of ye Veſtry		1700 & cask
For Ann Pallister		0400
For Mary Gordin		0400
For Capt Clayton Clr. of the County		0198
For Mr Boſwell Sheriff		0108
For the reverend Mr John Dixon's acct	£4‖19	0792
For John Tompkins's acct	7‖ 9	1192
For Docr Aſselins acct for Parrot	3‖11‖9	0588
For Thomas Rice		0500
For Capt Kemp Plummer his Acct		0122
For the widow Evans & four Children		1200
For Ann pallister & four Children		0600
For Elisabeth Baker for Jean. Hunley		0400
For Averill Bridge		0300
For John Riply for Do		0100
For Elenor Huts		0500
For John Bridge		0200
		27268

(35)	27268
For Lucy Summers	300
For Ann Lendal	500

For Capt Thomas Hayes for Oner Powers	250	
For Ann Lendal for D^{o}	750	
For George Hudgen for Keeping a Child	700	
For Mary Longeſt	300	
For Christian Owen	300	
For Elisabeth Bridge	300	
For the Church wardens to pay for Ornaments to be sent for By the Rever'd John Dixon if Not already sent for	10000	
for Robert Parrot for a levy over p^{d}	27½	
For Sarah wooden for D^{o}	27½	
For the Church wardens to pay for two Veſtry Houses 12 x 16 Fram'd & plaister'd and floored a Chimney & one window with Eight lights Robt parot to build one @ £7	2240	Tithables 1365
For John Hudgen	500	
	43463	34¼ lb Tobacco p^{r} pole
4 p^{r} Ct on 18900	756	
	44219	
6 p^{r} Ct for Collecting	2653	
	46872	

Ordered That Mr William Tabb & Capt Kemp Plummer Be Continued Church Wardens And that Mr William Tabb Do receive 34¼ pounds of Tobacco of Each Tithable Person in this Parish

Teſt John Dixon Junr Minis^{r}

(36)

Know all men by These Presents that We William Tabb & John Dixon Junior are held and firmly Bound unto the Gent^{m} of the Vestry of Kingstone Parish in the Sum of Ninety two Thousand Six hundred & fourty two pounds of Tobacco to be paid to The Said Vestrymen ——— or their succeſsors to the which Payment well and truly to be made we bind our Selves & Each of us our Heirs Executors and adminiſtrators Jointly and Severally firmly by these presents Sealed with our Seals and Dated this 22d Day of Octor 1753

Whereas the above bound William Tabb is appointed by the Veſtry of the pariſh of Kingston in the County of Glocesr to Collect and receive the Levy of the Said pariſh as the Same is aſsested on the 22d Day of Octor 1753. Now if the Said William Tabb Will Duly Collect pay and satisfie unto the several parish Creditors all the Tobacco for them respectively Levied then this obligation to be Void otherwiſe to be in full Force

Sealed & Deliver'd
In the preſents of — Wm Tabb
Francis Armistead — John Dixon Junr •
Hum'y Billups •

At a Vestry held for Kingston Pish ye 29 of May 1754
Prest Mr William Tabb Church warden, Mr William Armistead, Mr John Hayes Mr Thomas Hayes Mr Gwyn Reade, Mr Charles Debnam Mr Hugh Gwyn

Ordered that the Churchwardens Do pay mr William Armistead as much Tobacco as will pay his publick Dues to be deducted out of the Tobacco levied for Church ornaments

Order'd that the Church wardens have power to agree with workmen to repair the New Church as they think proper

Sign'd by Mr William Tabb Chh: wardn

(37)

Kingston parish ſs — At a Veſtry held for this Parish Novr: 26. 1754

The Reverend Mr John Dixon Minister
Mr William Tabb Capt Kemp Plummer Church Warden [ ]
Gentm Present Mr William Armistead Capt George Dudley Mr John Hayes Mr Charles Debnam Capt Gwyn Reade

Ordered that Tobacco be Levied as follows

To the Rever[d]. M[r] John Dixon Minister	16000 & Cask
To D[o] for Shrinkage 4 p[r] C[t]	640
To Ditto for Quitrents	128
To Thomas Dawson Clerk	1200
To John Davis Ditto & Clerk of Vestry	1700
To Ann Pallister Sexton	400
To Cap[t] John Clayton Clark of y[e] County	99
To Mary Gordin Sexton	400
To the widdow Evans & four Children	1200
To Ann Pallister for Keeping two Children	0600
To Elisabeth Baker for keeping Jean Hundley	400
To Averilla Bridge	400
To Elenor Huts	500
To John Bridge	200
To Lucy Summers	300
To Elisabeth Thomas for Keeping Oner Powers	1000
To George Hudgen for Keeping a Child	700
To Mary Longest widdow	500
To Christian Owen	400
To Elisabeth Bridge	300
To John Hudgen for Keeping a Child to be bound to him & his wife & to Clear the parish of it	1200
To Ann Pallister for Cleaning y[e] Church of the Whitewashing	100
To Sarah Merchant for Keeping her mother	500
To Thomas Jarrett	500
To Henry Knight for tobaco over paid Last year	205½
To Antony Degge jun[r] jun[r] for tobacco over paid Last Levy	68½
To M[r] Rob[t] Dalgeliſh for 15/ C[r] to Mary Bolton	120
(38)	
To the Reverend M[r] Dixon the Ballance of his acc[t]	1588
To John Rispoſs for Keeping Dorothy Jarrett	

seven months & half	0300
To Mr William Tabb for a bason for the New Church	32
To Thomas forrest for Keeping a Child of Lettitia Ashburys Seven weeks	150
To Richard Davis for two horse Blocks two horse racks a Door Case & Lintle & a Stand for Bason	1040
Robert Parret allow'd £1 more for building the Vestry House at the New Church	160
To John Tompkins Junr for Do at the old Church	160
To 4 ℘r Ct on 18900 for Cask	756
To William Tompkins Senr for work on the New Church	1120
	35067
6 ℘r C.t. on the whole for Collecting is 2104	2104
	37171

1379 Tithables   62 Deposr

Ordered that Capt. Gwyn Reade and Mr Charles Blacknall Do Stand Church wardens for the Ensueing year and yt Capt Gwyn Reade Do Recieve of Each Tithable Person in this Parish 27 pounds of Tobacco to sattisfie several creditors

Mr Charles Blacknall and Mr John Armistead Chosen Vestry men in the room of Major Ambrose Dudley and Mr. John Billups Deceas'd

Order'd that Samuel Willis be Levy free

Mr John Hayes this Day resigned his place of vestry man

Capt George Dudley this Day resigned his place of vestry man

memorandm That Thomas Forrest Keep the Child of Lettitia Ashburys till her return at the rate of 800lb of Tobacco ℘r Annum

Sign'd by the revernd Mr
John Dixon Minister

(39)

At a Vestry Held for Kingston Parish at the Old Church
July y[e] 18th 1755
The Rever'd M[r]. John Dixon Minis[r]

Pres[t].	Cap[tn] Gwyn Reade	M[r] Charles Blacknall
	Cap[t] Thomas Hayes	M[r] Charles Debnam
	Cap[t]. Kemp Plummer	M[r] William Tabb

Ordered That the Ballance in M[r] W[m] Tabbs hands of 27||6||4¼ be paid to M[r] William Armistead for the Church ornaments &c and that the Acc[t] be Settled at the Laying the Next Levy

Mem[d] That there has been paid to M[r] W[m] Armistead 5411[lbs] Toba[o] to be accounted for at 12/3½ ℔[r] C[t]

Ordered that the Church wardens have Power to agree with workmen to repair the old Church as they think proper

Order'd that the rever'd M[r] Dixon be Not Liable to Any Charge on acc[t] of the Negroe boys runing away that belongs to the parish

Teſtes John Dixon Jun[r] Minis[r]

(40)

Kingston Parriſh Sc At a Vestry held for this Piſh the 3[d] of Novem[r] 1755

Present

The Rever[nd] M[r] John Dixon Minis[r]

Cap[t] Gwyn Read	M[r] Charles Blacknall
Cap[t] Thomas Hayes	M[r] John Hayes
Cap[t]. Kemp Plummer	M[r]. Hugh Gwyn

M[r] Charles Debnam

Ordered That Toba[o] be Levied as follows Viz.

To The Rever[nd] M[r] Dixon Minister	16000 & cask
To D[o] for Shrinkage	.640
To D[o] for Quitrents	.128
To Thomas Dawson Clerk	1200 & cask
To John Davis D[o] & Clerk of Veſtry	1700 & cask

To Ann Pallister Sexton	.400
To Captn John Clayton Cl.k ye County	.117
To Mary Gordin Sexton	400
To Mary Evans widdow and four Children	1200
To Ann Pallister for keeping two Children	600
To Elisabeth Baker for Keeping Jane Hunley	400
To Averilla Bridge	400
To Elenor Huts	500
To John Bridge	400
To Lucy Summers	300
To George Hudgen for keeping a Child	700
To Mary Longest widdow	500
To Christian owen	400
To Elizabeth Bridg	300
To Sarah Merchant for keeping her Mother	500
To Thomas Jarrett	500
To Mr Matthew Whiting for Levies overpaid	61
To John Rispaſs for keeping Dorothy Jarrett	500
To Robert Reeves for keeping Oner powers	1000
To Thomas Forreſt for keeping a Child of Aſhberries	800
To the Sheriff	36
To Hannah fordom Widdow	300
To Mr Charles Blacknall	15
To John Callis	60
	30057

(41)

Bro^{t} over	30057
To Robert Hudgen Senier	258
To Robert Reade for Cloathing John Bolton	360
To Robert Dalgleish	56
To Robert Bridge	300
To John Huell for Levies over paid Last year	68½
To Mr William Armistead the Ballance of his acc^{t} £22‖11‖9 @ 2^{d} ℔^{r}	2710½
To The Rever,nd Mr John Dixon for Acc^{t}	

£9‖13‖7	1161½
To Doct^r John Symmer in part of Boltons Acc^t £15 @ 2^d	1800
To D^o. for Henry Carter £15 @ 2^d	1800
To 4 ℘^r C^t. on 18900 for Cask	756
	39327
To 6 ℘^r C^t on the whole for Collecting	2359
	41686

Ordered That Mr Charles Blacknall And Capt Gwyn Reade Continue Church Wardens for the Enſueing year — 1426 Tithables, 24 Depoſ^r.

Ordered That Mr Charles Blacknall Do Recieve of Each Tithable person in this Parriſh 29¼ ℘ounds Tobacco to Satisfie The Severall Creditors — 29¼ Each Tithab[ ]

Ordered that Ann Singletons Negro wench be Levy free

John Dixon Rect^r.

(42)

At a Veſtry Held for Kingston Pariſh the 10th Day of May 1756

The reverend Mr John Dixon Minis^r

Gent^m Pres^t
Capt Gwyn Reade
Mr Charles Blacknall — Churchwardens
Mr John Hayes
Mr Hugh Gwyn
Capt. Kemp Plummer
Mr William Tabb

Carried by a Majority that a Veſtry man be Now Choſen in the room of Mr William Armistead Deceas'd

Cap^tn William Plummer is Choſen to Succeed him as Veſtryman

Agreed that the reverend Mr Dixon May Saw into Plank or otherwise Diſpoſe of the trees felled on the Glebe for Neceſary Clearing Provided he Sell No board Timber

John Dixon. Junr. Rect^r.

(43)

At a Veſtry Held for Kingſton Parrish the 22[d] of Nov[r] In the year of our Lord 1756

Preſt. The Reverend M[r] John Dixon Miniſter
M[r] Charles Blacknall Capt. Gwyn Church wardens
M[r] William Tabb, M[r] Charles Debnam Cap[t]. Kemp Plummer M[r] John Hayes

Ordered That Toba[o] be Levied as follows

To The revern'd M[r] Dixon Miniſter	16000 & caſk
To D[o]. for Shrinkage	640
To D[o] for Quitrents	128
To Thomas Dawſon Clerk	1200 & caſk
To John Davis for D[o] & Clark of Veſtry	1700 & caſk
To Ann Pallister Sexton	400
To Mary Gordan Sexton	400
To Capt. John Clayton Cl[k]. of y[e] County	454
To M[r] Charles Tomkies Sheriff	72
To Elizabeth Evans & Two Children	800
To Ann Pallister for Keeping Two Children 3 months	150
To Elizabeth Baker for Keeping Jane Hundley	400
To Averilla Bridge	400
To Elenor Huts	500
To John Bridge	400
To Lucy Summers	300
To George Hudgen for Keeping a Child	700
To Deborah Edwards for Keeping Chriſtian Owen	400
To Elizabeth Bridge	300
To Sarah Merchant for Keeping her Mother	500
To Thomas Jarrett for Keeping his father	400
To Lewis Peed for Keeping Onner Powers	1000
To John Hudgen for Keeping y[e] Child of Aſh Berries	583
To Thomas Forreſt for Keeping y[e] Said Child two Months	117

To Richard Davis for clearing the New Church yard	100
To Hannah Fordom Widdow	300
To Robert Bridge	300
To George Mullens for taking Thomas Longeſt a Child of Mary Longeſt off ye P,iſh, & ye Child to be bound to him	800
To Izbel Parrett Widdow	300
Carried over	30194

(44)

To Acct Brought over	30194
For the reverend Mr John Dixon his his Acct. £10||13||2 to be paid in Tobao at 15/ ꝑr Ct	1420
To Mr Charles Blacknall for Acct.	277¾
To Joſeph King to be Lodged in the Church wardens hands till he has Complied with his agreemt. Viz £15||0||0 to be Deducted for an acct paid Mr Jameſon ꝑ Charles Blacknall £4||8||10½ £10||11||1½	1408
To be Left in the Church wardens hands till ordered out by the Veſtry for Repairs to the old Church	4000
6 pr Ct. on the whole for Collecting is	2283
4 pr Ct. on 18900 for Cask is 756	756
	40338

Capt. Kemp Plummer & Mr Hugh Gwyn Appointed Church-wardens for the Ensuing year

Order'd that Capt. Kemp Plummer Do receive of Each Tithable Perſon in this ꝑariſh 28 pounds of Tobao To Satiſfie The Several Creditors

Capt. William Plummer having Taken The Oaths according to law is admitted Veſtryman

Ordered That the Church wardens Do Endeavour to Procure a Deed for Land Sufficient for a Church yard at Each

Church from the Proprietors of the Land adjoining the Churches

1451 Tithab[ ] 28lb pr Tith[ ] Depofr 290

Sign'd By John Dixon Junr Rectr

(45)

I A B do ſwear that I will be faithfull & bear true Allegiance to his Majesty King George the ſecond so help me god

I A B do ſwear that I do from my heart Abhor detest and abjure as Impious & hereticall that Damnable doctrine and Poſition that Princes excommunicated or deprived by the Pope or any Authority of the ſee of Rome may be depoſed or Murthered by their Subjects or any other whatſoever & I do declare that no Forreign Prince Perſon Prelate state or Potentate hath or ought to have any Jurisdiction Power Superiority Preminence or Authority Ecclesiastical or Spiritual in this Realm so help me God

I A B do truly and sincerely acknowledge Profeſs teſtifie and declare in my conscience before God and the world that our Sovereign Lord King George the ſecond is Lawfull and Rightfull King of this Realm & of all other his Majesty's dominions and Countrys thereunto belonging and I do Solemnly & Sincerely declare that I do believe in my Conscience that the Person Pretended to be Prince of Wales during the life of the late King James and ſince his deceaſe Pretending to be and taking upon himſelf the ſtile and Title of King of England by the name of James the Third or of Scotland by the name of James the Eighth or the Stile & title of King of Great Britain hath not any right or title whatſoever to the Crown of this realm or any other the Dominions thereunto belonging & I do renounce refuſe & Abjure any Allegiance or Obedience to him and I do swear that I will bear faith and true Allegiance to his Majesty King George the ſecond & him will Defend to the Utmoſt of my power agst all traiterous

[illegible] and common sence & understanding of the same
[illegible] same words without [illegible] mental reservation [illegible]
[illegible] whatsoever and I do make this recognition Acknoledgement Abjuration renunciation & promise heartily
willingly and truly upon the true faith of a Christian

So help me God

[illegible] William [illegible] declare that [illegible]
[illegible] Sacrament of the Lord[illegible]
[illegible] or after the conse[illegible]
[illegible] whatsoever

William Plummer

1757 October 24th —— John Armistead

We the Subscribers will be conformable to ye Doctrin
& Discipline of the Church of England as it is now by Law
established.

Nov. 29. 1760

Thos Hayes
Kemp Plummer
Charles Blacknall
Wm Plummer
Jno Peyton
Wm Hayes
John Armistead
Thos Smith
Kemp Whiting
Wm Armistead
Edw. Hughes
[illegible] Willis
Thos Hayes

Page 46 of the Manuscript

Conſpiracies and Attempts whatſoever which shall be made againſt his Perſon Crown & Dignity & I will do my Utmoſt Endeavour to discloſe & make Known to his Majesty and his Succeſsors all treaſons and traiterous Conspiracys which I shall Know to be agst him or any of them & I do faithfully promiſe to the Utmoſt of my power to Support Maintain & defend the ſucceſsion of the Crown agst him the sd James and all other Perſons whatſoever as the ſame by an act Intituled an act for the further Limitation of the Crown and better Securing the rights and Liberties of the Subject is & stands Limited to the Princeſs Sophia Electoreſs and Dutcheſs Dowager of Hannover & the heirs of her body being Protestants and all these things I do truly and Sincerely Acknowledge according to the Expreſs words by me Spoken and (46) according to the Plain and Common ſense & Underſtanding of the ſame words without any Equivocation mental evation or Secret reſervation whatſoever and I do make this recognition Acknoledgement Abjuration renunciation & promiſe heartily willingly and truly upon the true faith of a Christian

So help me God

We whoſe names are here under Written do declare that we do believe that there is not any tranſubstantiation in the Sacrament of the Lords Supper or in the Elements of bread & wine at or after the Conſecration thereof by any Perſon whatſoever

William Plummer
1757 October 24th John Armistead

We the Subscribers will be conformable to ye Doctrine & Diſcipline of the Church of England as it is now by Law established

Thos Hayes
Kemp Plummer
Charles Blacknall
Novr 29. 1760 Wm Plummer
Jno Peyton

Wm Hayes
John Armistead
Thos: Smith
Kemp Whitinge
Wm Armistead
Edwd: Hughes
Jno Willis
Thos Hayes
(47) Geo: Dudley
Gabriel Hughes

(48)
Kingston Parrish — At a veſtry Held for this parriſh the 11th Day of April 1757

The Reverend Mr John Dixon Miniſter

Gentm Preſent		
	Capt George Dudley	Mr William Tabb
	Capt. Gwyn Reade	Mr Charles Debnam
	Mr John Hayes	Mr Charles Blacknall

This Day Mr Jefferson Dunbar Laid an acct before the Veſtry of £68||1||8¼ it is agreed by the Said veſtry That his work Materials &c. is worth No more than £40. which the Said veſtry agreed to give him but he refuſed to take it

To End the Diſpute the vestry and the Said Dunbar have agreed that Alexander Sanders Shall value the work and both Parties Shall abide by his Deciſion

John Dixon Jur. Recr

This day Mr Sanders & Mr Dunbarr met and Mr Sanders Measured the work &c & agreed that the work &c as ℘ acct is worth £51||12||7½

May 2th 1757 Chas: Blacknall

(49)
Kingston Piſh — At a Vestry Held for this pariſh Octobr 24th 1757

Present The Reverend Mr John Dixon Minister Mr Hugh Gwyn Capt George Dudley Capt Gwyn Reade Mr Charles Debnam Mr William Tabb Mr Charles Blacknall

Order'd Thatt Tobacco be Levied & paid as follows Viz.

To the rever'd Mr John Dixon Minisr	16000	& cask
To Do for Shrinkage	640	
To Do for Quitrents	128	
To Thomas Dawson Clk	1200	& cask
To John Davis Do & Clk of Veſtry	1700	& cask
To Ann Palister Sexton	400	
To Mary Gordan Sexton	400	
To Capt Clayton Clk County	48	
To Elizabeth Evans & two Children	800	
To Ann palisters heirs for keeping Jno Morgan	250	
To Elizabeth Baker for Keeping Jane Hundley	400	
To Elizabeth Baker for her Self	200	
To Avarilla Bride	400	
To Eleanor Huts	500	
To John Bridge to be paid to Mr Charles Blacknall	400	
To Lucy Summers	300	
To George Hudgen for Keeping a Child	700	
To Christian Owen	400	
To Elizabeth Bridge Widdow	300	
To Sarah Merchant for her Mother	500	
To Capt Thomas Hayes for Keeping Hon. powers	1000	
To John Davis for keeping Aſhbury's Child	450	
To Hannah Fordam	300	
To Robert Bridge	300	
To Isabella Parrot	300	
To Sarah White	500	
To Mary Bridge Widdow	500	
To Thomas Lewis Constable for services	258	
To Sarah Parrot for keeping a bastard Child 5 months	167	
To John Rispeſs for keeping Dorothy Jarrett	400	
	29841	
(50) Brought over	29841	
To John Davis for keeping Church Ornamts	200	

To Easter Hundley for Ann Craufords Children	200
To Capt Kemp Plummer for keeping a bastard Child	800
To the Churchwardens to Enable them to pay £24‖12‖7½ Being the Ballance Due to Jefferson Dunbar	4000
To the Rever'd Mr John Dixon for Wine and Land tax £3‖4s‖6d	461
To Do for paling 500 foot @ 3d £6‖5‖0	892
To Thomas Dawson for keeping plate. &c.	200
To Ann craford for her Children	300
	36894
To 4. pr. Ct. on 18900 is	756
	37650
To 6 ꝑ Ct. for collecting	2259
	39909

Mr Hugh Gwyn & Capt. Kemp Plummer continued Churchwardens

Ordered That Mr Hugh Gwyn Do recieve of Each Tithable person in this parish 27 lbs Tobao. the Number According to the List being 1481 78 Deposr.

Mr John Armistead took the oaths appointed By Law and is Admitted a Veſtryman

Ordered That that the collector pay Capt Thomas Hayes £1‖5s for the Negro boy in tobacco @ 14/ which comes to 178½

Capt John Peyton is appointed a Veſtryman in the room of Mr William Elliott Deceas'd

John Dixon Junr Rectr

(51)
Pariſh Kingston — At a Veſtry Held for this Pariſs Octobr. 23d. 1758

Present

The Reverd Mr John Dixon Minister

Mr Hugh Gwyn C. Kemp Plummer Churchwardens Mr John Hayes Mr Charles Debnam Capt. Thomas Hayes Mr Charles Blacknall C. Gwyn Reade Mr William Tabb Capt William Plummer Capt. John Peyton

Ordered that Tobacco be Levied as follows Viz.

To the Revd Mr John Dixon Minister	16000	& Cask
To Ditto for shrinkage	640	
To Ditto for Quitrents	128	
To Ditto for Wine and tax on the Glebe Land	502	
To Mr John Clayton Clk of the County	18	
To Thomas Dawſon Clk	1200	& caſk
To John Davis for Ditto & Clk of Veſtry	1700	& caſk
To Iſabella Parrett Sexton of the New Church	400	
To Mary Gordan Sexton of the old Church	400	
To Elizabeth Evans & two Children	800	
To Catharine Marwood for keeping Jane Hunley	400	
To Catharine Marwood for Keeping her Mother	200	
To Avarilla Bridge	400	
To Elenor Huts	500	
To John Bridge	400	
To Lucy Summers	300	
To Hudgen for Keeping a Lame Child	700	
To Chriſtian owen	400	
To Elizabeth Bridge Widdow	300	
To Sarah Merchant for Keeping her Mother to be paid to Mr Charles Blacknall	500	
To Captn Thomas Hayes for Keeping Oner Powers	1000	
To William Brounley for Keeping Joſeph Aſhbury	450	
To Hannah Fordam Widdow	300	
To John Bridge for Keeping & Burying His Father	300	
To Mary Bridge Widdow	200	
To John Riſpaſs for Keeping Dorothy Jarrett	400	

To John Davis for Keeping Church ornaments	200
To Wm Angel for Keeping a baſtard Child to be paid to M^r. Chas Blacknall	800
To Robert Parrett to take Gregory Crauford off the pariſh	1000
To D^o. for Keeping a Child of Ann Craufords	500
	31038

(52)

To Accompt Brought over	31038
To Sarah Baſset for her self	300
To Capt Gwyn Reade for Caſh & plank for Robt. Bridges Coffin	27
To William Chandler for Keeping a Baſtard Child 8 months	400
To Mr William Hayes for John Bolton his acc^t of 10||5||4 to be paid in tobacco @ 2^d ℔	1232
To Sarah Lovel	300
To 4 p^r C^t on 18900	756
	34053
To 6 p^r C^t. for Collecting	2043
	36096

Ordered That Capt William Plummer & Capt. John Peyton Do stand Church wardens for the Enſuing year

Ordered That Capt. John Peyton Do receive of Each Tithable Perſon in this Pariſh 25^lb Tobacco to Sattiſfie the several Creditors

Ordered that the Collector Do pay the Rever'd Mr John Dixon five Shillings & four pence out of the Depoſ^r & the Remains to Thomas Dawſon

Mr John Hayes Did this Day Reſign his place of Veſtryman

Ordered that Mr William Hayes & Mr Humphry Toye, Tabb is this Day Choſen veſtrymen in the room of Capt George Dudley Deceased & Mr John Hayes Reſign'd

(53)

At a Veſtry Held for Kingſton Pariſh The 5th Day of November in the year 1759

Preſent. The Rever'd M[r] John Dixon Minister
Capt. William Plummer, Capt. John Peyton Church wardens
Maj[r] Kemp Plummer M[r] William Tabb M[r] Charles Blacknall
M[r] Charles Debnam M[r] William Hayes Cap[t]. Thomas Hayes

Ordered That Tobacco be Levied as follows Viz.

To The Rev'd M[r] John Dixon	16000	& Caſk
To Ditto for Shrinkage	640	
To Ditto for Quitrents and Acco[t]	546	
To Thomas Dawson Clerk	1200	& Caſk
To John Davis Ditto & Cl[k] of Veſtry	1700	& Caſk
To Iſabel Parrot Sexton of the New Church	400	
To Mary Gordan Sexton of the old ditto	400	
To Thomas Dawſon for Keeping the Plate	200	
To Catherine Marwood for Keeping Jane Hunley	400	
To Averilla Bridge	400	
To Eleanor Huts Widow	500	
To John Bridge	400	
To Lucy Summers	300	
To Robert Hall for Keeping Hugh Brooks	600	
To Chriſtian Owen	400	
To Elizabeth Bridge Widow	300	
To Ann Brookes for Keeping Mary Bolton	500	
To Thomas Hayes for keeping & Burying oner powers	783½	
To William Brounley for Keeping Joſeph Aſhberry	450	
To Hannah fordam Widow	300	
To Mary Bridge Widow	200	
To Robert Sadler for Keeping Dorothy Jarrett	300	
To John Davis for Keeping Church Ornam[ts].	200	
To William Angel for Keeping a baſtard Child	400	
To Mary Flippen for Keeping Ann Craufords Child	450	

To Sarah Baʃset	300
	28269½

(54)

Brought over 28269½

To Aaron Hudgen for Keeping a baʃtard Child	600
To Wm Hayes for boarding John Bolton & Curing his Sore foot	1704
To Sarah Lovel Widow	400
To Thos Lewis Conʃtable for sundry Services	54
To Robert Hunley for a Coffin for Dorothy Jarrett	60
To Charles Blacknall for sundry Lawyers fees	540
To Joʃeph King for taring and painting the Veʃtry Houʃe and making fires therein During the Winter seaʃon	356
To Thomas Hayes for burying of Moʃes Owen and taking Care of his Widow in her sickneʃs	285
To Wm Plummer for two barryls Corn for Ann owen	150
To Wm Brounley for a Levy over paid laʃt year	25
To John Davis for making a fire in the veʃtry houʃe at the Lower Church	100
To Elizabeth Evens and two Children	800
To Suʃannah Sadler	300
To Robert Sadler for Burying Dorothy Jarrett	60
To Ann owen to be paid to Thos Hayes for Rent	200
To Suʃannah Driver and two Children	200
To Thomas Peak for keeping a baʃtard Child 2½ months at £7 ℔ Annum	175
To the Rever'd Mr Dixon for building a Quarter and Corn Houʃe on the Glebe	1341
4 ℔^r^ C^t^. on 18900	756
	36375½
6 ℔^r^ C^t^. for Collecting 2182	2182
Tithables 1450	38557½

(55)

Ordered That Wm Plummer and John Peyton Gentm be continued Churchwardens the Enſueing year and that Wm Plummer Gent be appointed to collect of Each Tithable Perſon in this Pariſh twenty six Pounds & half of Tobacco to satiſfy the several creditors

Ordered That the Pariſh be divided into the uſual Precincts and that such Perſons as the Church wardens Name in each precinct be Proceſsioners

Ordered That John Peyton Gentm do pay to the Rev'd Mr Dixon the ballance which now remains in his hands of the Last Collection

Ordered That a well built Quarter Twenty Feet long & sixteen feet wide; and a corn Houſe Sixteen Feet long & twelve Feet wide be built at the Glebe by the Rev'd Mr Dixon for Which he is to be allow'd one Thousand five hundred pounds of Tobacco

(56)

At a Veſtry Held for Kingſton Pariſh Novr 29th 1760
Preſent The Rev'd Mr John Dixon Minister
Capt. William Plummer Capt John Peyton Church Wardens
Capt. Thomas Hayes, Majr Kemp Plummer Mr Charles Blacknall Mr William Hayes Gentm of the Veſtry

Ordered That Tobacco be Levied as follows Viz.

To the reverend Mr John Dixon Minisr	16000	& cask
To ditto for Shrinkage	640	
To ditto for Quitrents and accompt for Wine	528	
To Capt John Clayton Clerk of the County	18	
To Thos. Dawſon Clerk	1200	& cask
To John Davis Clerk of Church & Veſtry	1700	& cask
To Iſabella Parrot Sexton of the New Church	400	
To John Davis Ditto of the old Church	400	
To Thomas Dawſon for Keeping the Plate	200	
To Catharine Marwood for Keeping Jane Hunley	400	
To Averilla Bridge	400	

To Judith Machen for Keeping Eleanor Huts	500
To Thomas Peak for John Bridge	400
To Rich[d] Summers for Keeping his mother 2 months in sickneſs	150
To Rob[t] Reaves for keeping Lucy summers some time & burying her	150
To Rob[t] Hall for keeping Hugh Brookes	600
To Chriſtian owen	400
To Elizabeth Bride Widow	500
To Ann Brookes for keeping Mary Bolton	500
To William Brownley for Keeping Joſeph Aſhbury	450
To Hannah Fordam widow	300
To John Davis for keeping Church orments	200
To W[m] Angel for keeping a baſtard Child, To be paid to Langley Billups	400
To Mary Flippen for keeping Ann Craufords Child	450
To Sarah Baſsett	300
To Sarah Lovel Widow	400
To Iſabella Parrott for Keeping the upper Veſtry Houſe in good order	100
To John Davis Keeping the Lower ditto in good order	100
To Elizabeth Evans two Hundred & her son to be bound out	200
To Suſannah Sadler for keeping Her lame Daughter	300
To Ann owen to be paid to Capt. Thomas Hayes for Rent	200

(57)

To Acc[t] brought over	
To the Rev'd John Dixon a farther allowance for the quarter	286
To accompt not levied laſt year for the Rev'd M[r] John Dixon	86

To Suſannah Driver for Keeping her two Children	300
To Robt Hunley for making a Coffin for Eleanor Huts	60
To Robt Hall for taking Hugh Brookes off the Pariſh	600
To 4 pr Ct. on 18900 allow'd for caſk	756
	30574
To 6 pr Ct. for Collecting	1834
	32408

Ordered that Capt, William Hayes and Capt, Thomas Hayes do stand Church wardens for the Enſueing year

Ordered That Capt William Hayes do receive of Each Tithable Perſon in this Pariſh 22½ pounds of Tobacco to Satiſfy the Several creditors there being 1481 Tithables in the liſt there remaining 914 to be accounted for by the Collector

This Day Capt Gwyn Read by Letter to the Gentm of veſtry Does reſign his place of veſtryman

Ordered Capt. Thomas Smith Mr Kemp Whiting and Mr George Dudley be choſen veſtrymen, in the room of Mr Charles Debnam Deceas'd Mr Humpy. Toye Tabb Deceas'd and Capt Gwyn Reade Reſign'd

Teſt John Davis

(58)

At a Veſtry Held for Kingſton Pariſh Novr 9th 1761

The Rev'd Mr John Dixon Miniſter, Capt Thos Hayes Church Warden Majr Kemp Plummer Mr Charles Blacknall, Mr Kemp Whiting Mr Wm Plummer Mr Thos Smith Mr John Armiſtead

Ordered That Tobacco be levied as follows Viz.

To the Rev'd Mr John Dixon Minister	16000 & caſk
To ditto for Shrinkage	640
To ditto for quitrents & acct	720

To Capt John Clayton Cl^{k} of the County	54
To John Davis Cl^{k} of the lower Church & veſtry	1700 & caſk
To Thos Dawſon Cl^{k} of the upper Church	1200 & caſk
To Iſabella Parrett Sexton of the upper Church	400
To John Davis ditto of the old Church	400
To Thos Dawſon for Keeping the Plate	200
To Catherine Marwood for Keeping Jane Hunley	400
To Averilla Bridge	400
To John owen for his Siſter Chriſtian owen & burying her	400
To Elizabeth Bridge widow	500
To Mary Bolton	500
To William Brownley for keeping Joſeph Aſhbery	350
To hannah Fordom Widow	300
To John Davis for Keeping Church ornaments	200
To Mary Flippen for Keeping ann Craufords Child	400
To Sarah Baſset	300
To John Davis for keeping the lower veſtry Houſe	100
To Thos. Dawſon	48
To Iſabella Parrett for keeping the upper veſ^{y} Houſe	100
To Suſanna Sadler for keeping her lame Daugh^{r}	300
To Ann owen Widow to be paid to Capt Thomas Hayes	200
To Elizabeth Green widow	500
To Joanna Barnett widow & Children	300
To Mary Baxter widow	500
To Wm Angel for keeping a baſtard Child	400

(59)

To Henry Powel for looking after a ſick man & burying him	300
To John Buſh	250

To 4 ℔r Ct. on 18900 for caſk	756
To be left in the hands of the Church wardens towards Repairing the Glebe houſe & building a room 16 x 20 with brick and a Brick Chimney	5000
	33818
To 6 ℔r Ct. on the whole for collecting	2029
	35847

Ordered That the Church wardens have Power to agree with workmen to build a gallery in the old Church

Ordered That Capt. Thomas Hayes & Capt. William Hayes Do Stand Church wardens for the Enſueing year

Ordered that Capt. Thomas Hayes do receive of Each Tithable Perſon in this Pariſh 24½ lb Tobacco to sattiſfy the several Creditors there being 1486 tithables on the liſt

Memorandm That Mr Hugh Gwyn By Meſsage to the veſtry Reſigns his Place of of veſtryman which if he confirms under his hand Mr Edward Hughes is agreed to be Choſen in his room

Witneſs John Davis Clk V.

(60)

At a veſtry Held for Kingſton Pariſh Novr 1st. 1762

Preſent, The Reverend Mr John Dixon Miniſter Capt. Thos Hayes Capt William Hayes Churchwardens, Maj.'r Kemp Plummer Mr William Tabb Capt. William Plummer, Capt. John Peyton Capt. Thomas Smith Mr Kemp Whiting Mr George Dudley

Ordered That Tobacco be levied as follows Viz.

To the Rever'd Mr John Dixon Miniſter	16000 & caſk
To Do for Shrinkage	640
To Do for Quitrents and acct	645
To Capt John Clayton Clk of the Court	18
To John Davis Clk of the Lower Church & Veſtry	1700 & cask

To Thomas Dawſon Clerk of the upper Church	1200 & caſk
To Iſabella Parrett Sexton of the upper Church	400
To John Davis sexton of the Lower Church	400
To Thomas Dawſon for Keeping the Plate	200
To Catherine Marwood for Keeping Jane Hunley	400
To Averilla Bridge	400
To Elizabeth Bridge Widow	500
To Mary Bolton	600
To Hannah	400
To John Davis for Keeping Church ornamts Cuſhions &c	200
To Sarah Baſset Widow	300
To John Davis for making fires in the Lower veſtry houſe	100
To Iſabell Parret for do of the upper veſtry houſe	100
To Ann owen, to be paid to Capt. Thos Hayes for rent	200
To Suſanna Sadler for Keeping her lame Daughter	300
To Elizabeth Green Widow	500
To Joanna Barnet and Children	300
To Mary Baxter Widow	500
To William Angel for taking the Child off the Pariſh that he has formerly kept	200
To John Buſh	250
To Suſannah Sadler for keeping Thos Thurſtons Child	200
To Robt Hudgen	400
	27053

(61)

To Acct Brought up	27053
To Majr Kem Plummer for a levy over paid last year	24½
To Capt Wm Plummer for a levy over Charged	26½
To Matthew Gayle for two Levies over	

charged	49
To Aaron Hudgen for keeping a Child 7 months	350
To Capt. Wm Hayes to Ballance of His acct.	676
To be left in the Churchwardens hands to pay Mr Jefferson Dunbar for Building on the Glebe &c. and Gallery in the Church	10000
To Auguſtine Degge for Levies over paid laſt year	122½
To 4 ℘ Ct. on 18900 allow'd for cask	756
	*39063½
To 6 ℘ Ct for Collecting	2343
	41406½

1424 Tithable[ ] 208 Depoſr after J. Deg[ ] is paid 400 for Wm ange[ ]

Ordered That Capt Thomas Smith and Mr Kemp Whiting do Stand Churchwardens for the enſueing year

Ordered That Capt Thos Smith Do receive of each Tithable Perſon in this Pariſh 29½ lbs. of Tobacco to sattiſfy the several Criditors

Ordered That the collector Do pay Joſeph Degge for Wm Angel 400 lb Tobacco out of the Deposr and acct for the reſt at the laying of our next levy

Ordered that Mr Edward Hughes & Mr James Ranſone Be choſen Veſtrymen in the room of Mr Charles Blacknall and Mr John Armistead Deceas'd

ordered That Moſes Hudgen and Richard Machen be levy free

Witneſs John Davis

* The original addition was 39063½. Later the two last digits were overwritten with a 5 and a 7 respectively, and the total then read 39057½; but no corresponding change was made in the final total, 41406½.—C. G. C.

(62)

At a Veſtry Held for Kingſton Pariſh Nov[r] 28th 1763
Preſent, The Rever'd M[r] John Dixon Miniſter

Capt. Thomas Smith, M[r] Kemp Whiting Church wardens, Capt William Hayes, Capt. John Peyton, Maj,r Kemp Plummer, M[r] William Tabb, M[r] George Dudley, Capt Thomas Hayes, M[r] James Ranſone.

Ordered That Toba[o] be Levied as follows Viz.

To the Rev'd M[r]. John Dixon Miniſter	16000 & cask
To Ditto for Shrinkage	640
To ditto for quitrence and acc[t]	630
To Capt. John Clayton Cl[k] of y[e] County Court	18
To John Davis Cl[k] of the Lower Church & veſtry	1700 & cask
To Tho[s] Dawſon d[o] of the New Church	1200 & cask
To Iſabella Parrett Sexton of the New Church	400
To John Davis d[o] of the old Church	400
To Thomas Dawson for Keeping the Plate	200
To Catherine Marwood for keeping Jane Hunley	400
To Mary Bolton	600
To Hannah Fordom	400
To John Davis for keeping Church ornam[ts] Cuſhions &c	200
To Sarah Baſset	400
To Iſabella Parrett for making fires in the upper veſtry houſe	100
To John Davis for ditto of the lower veſtry House	100
To Ann Owen to be paid to Capt. Thomas Hayes for Rent	200
To Elizabeth Bridge Widow	500
To Elizabeth Green widow and Small Children	500
To Joanna Barnett widow and small Children	300
To Mary Baxter	500
To Suſann Sadler for keeping Tho[s] Thurſtons Child	200
To John Buſh	250

To Sufannah Sadler for keeping her Daugh[r] having fits & lame	500
To Langley Billups for 2 levies not receivd	49
To Doc[r] John Symmer for John Bufhes wife and Ann Burton	871½
To Ann Owen Allow'd to build her an house	400
To Capt. William Hayes on acc[t] of Ann Burton	432
To M[r] Rob[t] Dalgleifh for Tho[s] Newburn on acc[t]. Averilla Bridge	200
To Rob[t] Hall to take Tho[s] Thurftons Child off the Parifh	500
	28790

(63)

To Acc[t]. Bro[t]. over	28790
To be left in the Church wardens hand towards paying off M[r] Jefferson Dunbars acc[t]	4483
To be left in the Church wardens Hands toward repairing the old Church	2500
To Whenefred Longeft	500
To 4 p[r]. C.t. on 18900 for Cask	756
	37029
To 6 p[r]. C[t]. for Collecting	2221
	39250

Ordered That Capt. Thomas Smith and M[r] Kemp Whiting do Stand Church wardens for the Enfueing year

Ordered That M[r]. Kemp Whiting do receive of each Tithable perfon in this Parifh 25½[lb] Toba[o] to Satiffy the several Creditors

This day M[r] William Tabb Refign'd his place of veftryman

Ordered That M[r] Robt Tabb have notice that he is Chofen veftryman In the room of M[r] William Tabb Refignd

Tiths for the year 1763 1552 Depof[r]. 326

Teft John Davis Cl[k]

At a Veſtry held for Kingſton Pariſh aug[t]. 15 1763
Preſent, The Rev'd M[r]. John Dixon Miniſter

Cap[t] Tho[s] Smith, M[r] Kemp Whiting, Churchwardens Capt. Tho[s] Hayes, Maj[r] Kemp Plummer, M[r] William Tabb Capt. William Hayes, Cap[t] John Peyton, M[r] George Dudley M[r]. Edward Hughes, M[r] James Ranſone,

Ordered That the Church wardens get three Windows put into the Church and have the beam cut away and and get the Pews mended and any other small Repairs they Shall Think Neceſsary

Reſolvd that Jefferson Dunbar has not compleated the plaiſtering of the Gallery in a workmanlike manner

Teſt John Davis

(64)

At a veſtry Held for Kingſton Pariſh Nov[r]. 19th in the year 1764

Preſent The rev'd M[r]. John Dixon Miniſ[r]

Capt. Thomas Smith M[r] Kemp Whiting Church warden Capt. Tho[s] Hayes, Capt W[m] Hayes, C, John Peyton, M[r] George Dudley M[r] Edward Hughes M[r] James Ranſone Maj[r] Kemp Plummer

Ordered That Tobacco be levied as follows Viz.

To the rev'd M[r] John Dixon Miniſ[r]	16000	& cask
To ditto for Shrinkage	640	
To ditto for Quitrence & accompt	700	
To Capt. John Clayton Cl[k]	18	
To John Davis Clk. of lower Church & veſtry	1700	& cask
To Tho[s] Dawson Ditto of the New Church	1200	& cask
To Iſabella Parrett Sexton of the New Church	400	
To John Davis ditto of the old Church	400	
To Tho[s] Dawſon for Keeping the plate	200	
To Catherine marwood for Keeping Jane Hunley	400	
To Mary Bolton	600	
To Hannah Fordom	400	

To John Davis for Keeping John Davis for Keeping Church Ornaments Cuſhions &c 200
To Sarah Baſset 400
To Iſabella Parrott for making fires in the upper Veſtry Houſe 100
To John Davis for d° of the lower veſtry houſe 100
To Ann Owen for rent to be paid to C. Thos Hayes 200
To Elizabeth Bridge Widow 600
To Elizabeth Green Widow 500
To Joannah Barnett and Small Children 300
To Mary Baxter 500
To Suſannah Sadler for keeping Daughter having fits and Lame 500
To John Ripley for 1 levy over paid laſt year 25½
To Thos pool for one levy over paid laſt year & 1 this year 55
To Mr Gabriel Hughes to finish Ann Owens Houſe 366
To Wm Blake to his Ballance 680
To The Rev'd Mr John Dixon to pay Jefferson Dunbar 18||9||9 2464
[ ]rs Mary Tabb for for Elizabeth Lovet 533

(65)

To acct brot up
To Elizabeth Turner and Small Children 500
To Thomas Newburn for a year to come Keeping Elizabeth Parrots Bastard 500
To 4. ℔r Ct. on 18900 for cask 756
To 6. ℔r Ct for Collecting

Orererd That Mr. Kemp Whiting do pay 11||7||1 out of the money in his hands to Wm Blake
and also 20||7||3 to
Jefferson Dunbar

Ordered That James Howgate & Thomas Williams be Levy free

Ordered That Mr George Dudley and Mr Edward Hughes be appointed Church Wardens, and Mr George Dudley is authorized to receive twenty three pounds of Tobacco for each Tithable perſon in this pariſh

Ordered That two Dials preſented to the pariſh by the Rev'd John Dixon be fixed up on Subſtantial and neat poſts of Cedar Locuſt or Mulberry to be paid for out of the Tobo left in the Collectors hands being 532 lbs.

Ordered. That what shall be left in the Collectors hands after putting up the Dials and alſo 326lb of Tobo in Mr Kemp Whitings Hands be paid to Mr Robert Billups for maintaining Elizabeth Hooks Baſtard But the Church wardens are Deſired to bring suit againſt the father of the Child, and Proſecute the Woman, and all others who have Baſtards for the Fine

Teſt John Davis.

(66)

At a Veſtry Held for Kingſton Pariſh Octobr 28th 1765

Present The Rev'd Mr John Dixon Miniſr

Mr George Dudley, Mr Edward Hughes Church Wardens Capt. William Hayes Capt, John Peyton Mr Kemp Whiting Mr James Ranſone, Mr Robert Tabb, Capt Thos, Hayes

Ordered That Tobacco be Levied as follows Viz.

To The Rev'd Mr John Dixon Miniſter	16000 & cask
To ditto for Shrinkage	640
To ditto for quitrents and acct of 4||15||3	476
To Capt John Clayton Clerk of the County Court	265½
To John Davis Clerk of ye Lower Church & Veſtry	1700 & cask
To Thomas Dawſon Clerk of the New Church	1200 & cask
To Iſsabella Parrett Sexton of the New Church	400
To John Davis sexton of the old do	400
To Thomas Dawſon for keeping the plate	200
To Catherine Marwood for keeping Jane Hunley	400
To Mary Bolton	600

To Hannah Fordom Widow	400
To John Davis for keeping Church ornaments Cuſhions &c, & Making fires in the Veſtry Houſe	300
To Iſsabella Parrett for making fires in the upper Veſtry Houſe	100
To Sarah Baſset Widow	400
To Ann Owen to be paid to Capt. Thos Hayes for Rent	200
To Elizabeth Bridge Widow	600
To Elizabeth Green Widow	400
To Joanna Barnett Widow & Children	300
To Mary Baxter Widow	500
To Suſannah Sadler for Keeping her Lame Daughter	500
To Elizabeth Turner Widow & Children	500
To Judith Machen Widow	200
To George Mullins for taking James Lovt son of Elizabeth Lovet off the Pariſh	1200
To Richard Sumers for Burying Richard Buſh	100
	27981½

(67)

To Acct. Brought over	27981½
To Iſsabella Parrett to Enable her to keep Elizabeth Parrets Child the Enſueing year	400
To Mr, Peter Bernard for Delinquents	230
To Mr George Dudley for 3/9 Paid for Writs	18½
To Docr Georg Johnſon to pay 3||15||11 Curing Wheneford Longeſts Leg	378
To Judith Miller Towards Building her houſe	500
To Jane Reaves	300
To Mr Gabriel Hughes	37
To 4 ℔ Ct on 18900 for caſk	756
	30601
To 6 ℔ Ct for Collecting	1836
	32437

Ordered That Mr George Dudley and Mr Edward Hughes Do stand Church wardens for the Enſueing year

Ordered That Mr Langley Billups Do receive of Each Tithable perſon in this Pariſh 22¼ lbs Tobacco to sattiſfy the several Creditors

Ordered That Mr Langley Billups do acct for the remainder of 222 lbs Tobao at the Laying the Next Pariſh Levy

Witneſs John Davis

(68)

At a Veſtry Held for Kingſton Pariſh Novr 18th. 1766

Preſent The Rev'd Mr. John Dixon Miniſter

Mr. Edward Hughes, Mr George Dudley, Church wardens Capt Thomas Hayes, Capt William Hayes Capt. Thomas Smith Mr James Ranſone, Mr Robert Tabb, Majr William Plummer

Ordered That Tobacco be levied as follows Viz

To the Rev'd Mr John Dixon Miniſter	1600 & caſk
To do for Shrinkage	640
To Ditto for Quitrents & wine £4‖15‖3	549
To Capt John Clayton	18
To John Davis Clerk of ye Lower Church & Veſtry	1700 & cask
To Thomas Dawſon Clerk of the New Church	1200 & caſk
To Iſsabella Parrett Sexton of the New Church	400
To John Davis do of the old Church	400
To Catherine Marwood for keeping Jane Hunley	400
To Thos Dawſon for keeping the Plate	200
To Mary Bolton	600
To Hannah Fordom Widow	400
To Jno Davis for keeping Church ornamts. Cuſhions &c & making fires in the Veſtry Houſe	300
To Iſsabella Parrett for making fires in the upper Veſtry Houſe	100
To Sarah Baſset widow	400
To Ann Owen	200

To Elizabeth Bridge	600
To Elizabeth Green widow	200
To Mary Baxter	500
To Elizabeth Turner Widow & Children	300
To Judith Machen Widow	200
To Jane Reaves Widow, to be paid to Wm Anderton	300
To Suſannah Sadler for keeping her Daughter being lame & having fits	500
To 4 ℘^{r} C^{t} on 18900 for cask	756
	26863

(69)

To acc^{t} bro^{t} up	26863
To Richard Morgan & his Wife	300
To Martha Chriſtian Widow & Children	400
To John Soper	500
To Elias Pew to Enable him to School a Child two years	250
To Joſeph Tabor for keeping Elizabeth Soles Child Six months paſt	300
To Mr George Dudley for Cutting Pines in the New Church Yard	50
To Mr Langley Billups for Ball^{ce} of Levies Over Charg'd Laſt year	84½
To be Paid to the Church wardens for Clothing Hugh Brookes	200
To Thomas Williams towards Clothing him	300
To Mrs Mary Blacknall to Enable her to keep Ann Colemons Child the Enſuing year	300
To the Rev'd Mr John Dixon for Pailing the Garden and Covering the Cellar and Stable and finding all	1350
	30897
To 6 ℘ C^{t}. for Collecting	1853
	32750

Ordered That Mr Robert Tabb and Mr James Ranſone Act as Church wardens the Enſueing year

Ordered that Mr Langley Billups be appointed Collector and that he Receive of Each Titheable Perſon in this Parish the sum of Twenty two Pounds of Toba° to Satiſfy the several Creditors above mentioned

Sign'd by the Rev'd Mr John Dixon

Witneſs John Davis

At a Veſtry Held for Kingſton Pariſh Septr 28th 1767

Preſent The Rev'd Mr John Dixon Miniſter

Majr Kemp Plummer Majr William Plummer Capt. John Peyton Capt. Thomas Smith Capt Wm Hayes Mr Kemp Whiting Mr. George Dudley Mr Robt Tabb

Ordered that Mr William Armistead of Heſse be appointed veſtry man in the Room of Mr James Ranſone Decea'd

Witneſs John Davis

(70)

At a Veſtry Held for Kingſton Pariſh Novr 23d 1767

Preſent The Revd Mr John Dixon Miniſter Capt. Thos. Hayes Majr. Kemp Plummer Capt. Wm Hayes Capt John Peyton Mr George Dudley Mr. Kemp Whiting, Mr Edward Hughes Capt Thomas Smith

Ordered That Tobacco be levied as follows

To the Rev'd Mr John Dixon Miniſter	16000 & cask
To ditto for Shrinkage	640
To ditto for Quitrents and acct £4‖15‖3	476
To be paid for Copy of the Liſt of Tithables	18
To John Davis Clark of the Lower Church & veſtry	1700 & caſk
To Thomas Dawſon Clk of the New Church	1200 & caſk
To Iſabella Parot Sexton of the New Church	400
To Jno Davis ditto of the old Church	400
To Catherine Marwood for keeping Jane Hunley	400
To Thomas Dawſon for keeping the Plate	200

To Mary Bolton	600
To Hannah Fordom Widow	400
To Jno Davis for Keeping Church ornam^{ts} Cuſhions &c and making fires in the Lower Veſtry Houſe	300
To Sarah Baſset Widow	400
To Elizabeth Bridge Widow	600
To Ann Owen Widow	200
To Mary Baxter	500
To Elizabeth Turner Widow and Children	300
To Judith Machen Widow	300
To Jane Reaves Widow	300
To Suſanna Sadler for keeping her Lame Daughter	500
To Richard Morgan and his Wife	300
To Martha Chriſtian Widow & Children	400
To Mrs Ann Blacknall for keeping Ann Colemans Child	300
To Richard Longeſt for Keeping Dorothy Parrots Child the year Laſt paſt; to be paid to the Rev'^{d} John Dixon	600
To Joſeph Tabor for Keeping the Child of Elizabeth Soles The year laſt paſt to be paid to Mr Langley Billups	600
(71)	
Brought over	28034
To Suſannah Sadler	100
To Moſes Hudgen for a Levy over paid laſt year	22
To James Huggate	200
To Joſeph King 5^{s}/	25
To Mr Robert Dalgeiſh 10/	50
To 4 ꝑ C^{t}. on 18900 for Caſk	756
To Iſsabella Parrot for making fires in the Veſtry Houſe at the New Church	100
To Henry Hunley for 3 Levies over paid laſt year	66

To Wilkinſon Hunley for 10 ditto	220
To Deborah Edwards widow	300
To Mr Langley Billups for Tithables given him in the Laſt year that he cant receive Levies from	564
	30437
To 6 ℘ Ct. for Collecting	1826
	32263

Ordered That Mr Robert Tabb do receive of each Tithable Perſon in this Pariſh 21 lbs of Tobacco to Sattiſfy the Several Creditors

Ordered That Capt John Peyton do Stand Churchwarden for the Enſueing year With Mr Robert Tabb

Signed by The Rev'd Mr John Dixon

Witneſs John Davis

(72)

At a Veſtry Held for Kingſton Pariſh Decr 12th 1768

Preſent The Rev'd Mr John Dixon Miniſr Mr Robt. Tabb Capt John Peyton, Churchwardens Capt Wm Hayes Mr Kemp Whiting Mr George Dudley Mr Edward Hughes Capt. Thomas Smith

Ordered That Tobacco be Levied as follows Viz.

To The Rev'd Mr John Dixon Miniſter	16000 & cask
To do for Shrinkage	640
To Capt John Clayton for Copy of Liſt of Tithables	18
572 To The rev'd Mr John Dixon for Quitrents & wine £4‖15s‖5d	572
To John Davis Clerk of ye old Church	1700 & cask
To Thomas Dawſon do of the New Church	1200 & cask
To Iſsabella Parret sexton of the New Church	400
To John Davis ditto of the old Church	400
To Catherine Marwood for Keeping Jane Hunley	400
To Thomas Dawſon for keeping the plate	200

To Mary Bolton Widow to be paid to Robert Cully	600
To Hannah Fordam Widow	400
To John Davis for keeping Church ornam[ts] Cuſhions &c	200
To John Davis for making fires in the Veſtry Houſe	100
To Iſsabella Parrett for making fires in the upper ditto	100
To Sarah Baſset Widow	400
To Elizabeth Bridge Widow	600
To Ann Owen Widow to be paid to Cap[t] Tho[s] Hayes	200
To Elizabeth Turner Widow and Children	300
To Judith Machen Widow & Children	300
To Jane Reaves Widow to be paid to William Ander[ton]	300
To Suſanna Sadler for her Lame Daughter	500
To Richard Morgan and Wife	300
To Martha Chriſtian Widow & Children	400
To Richard Longeſt for keeing Dorothy Parets Child	500
To Mrs Mary Blacknall for keeping ann Cole-mãs Child	400
To Joſeph Tabor for keeping Elizabeth Soles's Child To be paid to Langley Billups	400
To James Hugget	200
To Deborah Edwards Widow	300
	28030

(73)

To Acc[t] Bro[t] up	28030
To 4 ℔ C[t]. on 18900 for Cask	756
To be left in the Church wardens Hands to-wards paying the Doctors for John Soper	1200
To Ann King Widow and Children	300
To M[r] Richard Gregory for proviſion for S[d]	

Ann King	250
To Joſhua Bridge for a wons Lying in and board at his house seven weeks to be paid to Fran^s Miller	150
To Mr John Billups for Corn for Elizabeth Treacle	150
To Mr Robert Tabb for 19 Tithables that he cannot Receive Levies from	399
To The Rev'd Mr John Dixon for Building a Quarter on the Glebe £40	4000
To ditto for an Houſe for the Overſeer 16 x 12 £5	500
To ditto for repairing the Veſtry Houſe at the old Church	200
	35935
To 6 ℔ C for Collecting	2156
	38091

Ordered That Mr Charles Tompkies Sheriff do Collect and Receive of each Tithable perſon in this Pariſh 24¼ lbs of Tobacco to sattiſfy the several Pariſh Creditors

Ordered That Mr William Armistead stand Church warden the Enſueing year with Sir. John Peyton

Ordered That Capt Francis Armistead Have Notice That he is Choſen Veſtryman in Stead of Mr Hugh Gwyn Resign'd

Teſt John Davis

(74)

At a Veſtry Held for Kingſton Pariſh Decr 11th 1769

Preſent The Rev'd Mr John Dixon Minister

Sir John Peyton William Armistead Gent^m Church Wardens Capt. William Hayes, Capt. Thos. Smith, Mr Edward Hughes, M^r. Robert Tabb M^r. George Dudley

Ordered That Tobacco be Levied as follows Viz.

To The Rever'd Mr John Dixon Minister 16000 & cask

To Ditto for Shrinkage	640	
To Ditto for Quitrents and acct	1615	
To Capt. John Clayton for Copy of the Liſt Tithables	18	
To John Davis Clk of Church & Veſtry	1700	& cask
To Ditto Sexton of old Church	400	
To Ditto for keeping Church Ornaments Cuſh-ions &c	200	
To Ditto for making fires in thie Lower Veſtry Houſe	100	
To Thomas Dawſon Clerk of the New Church	1200	& cask
To Ditto for keeping the Plate	200	
To Robert Sadler & Ann King Sextons of New Church	400	
To Ditto for keeping fires in the Veſtry Houſe	100	
To Catherine Marwood for keeping Jane Hunley	400	
To Mary Bolton	600	
To Sarah Baſset Widow	400	
To Elizabeth Bridge Widow	600	
To Ann Owen Widow to be paid to C. Thos Hayes	200	
To Elizabeth Turner Widow & Children	300	
To Judith Machen	300	
To Jane Reaves Widow	300	
To Suſannah Sadler for keeping her lame Daughter	500	
To Richard Morgan & Wife	300	
To Martha Chriſtian Widow & Children	400	
To James Hugget	200	
To Deborah Edwards Widow	300	
To Joſeph Tabor for keeping & burying Eliza Soles Child	400	
To Richard Longeſt for keeping keeping Dor-othy Parrets Child, to be paid to Thomas Flippen	500	
	28273	

(75)

To Acc^t Brought up	28273
To Ann King Widow & Children	300
To Richard Morgan to buy Provision for this time only	500
To John Brownley	300
To John Sampson	300
To Elizabeth Brownley and Children	600
To be paid Sir John Peyton for Doctor Thos Clayton on acct of Elizabeth Parrett	508
To Joanna Barnett Widow & Children	300
To Richard Gregory for a Coffin for Elizabeth Lovet	50
To Mary Chambers for Laying and boarding Mildred Bridges	150
To James Hodges for 2 Levies over paid	42
To James Harris for making a Coffin for Hannah Fordom	50
To Elizabeth Trekle Widow	400
To 4 ℔ Ct on 18900 for Cask	756
To Mr. Charles Tompkies for Insolvents	1081
	33610
To 6 ℔r Ct for Collecting	2016½
	35626

Number of Tithables on the List from the from the office is with the addition of some more found out by the Vestry 1421 Levy ℔r pole 25 lb Remainder 101 lb Toba°

Ordered That William Armistead Gentm and Sir John Peyton stand Church Wardens the Ensueing year

Ordered that Mr Langley Billups do receive of each Tithable Person in this Parish 25 lbs Tobacco to Sattisfy the several Parish Creditors and to acct for the remainder at Laying the next Levy for this Parish

Ordered That Mr. John Willis have notice that the vestry have Chosen him vestryman in the room of Capt. Thos Hayes who this day by note to the veſtry reſign'd his place of Veſtryman.

It is the Opinion of the Veſtry that the Church wardens ought to rectify any mistake that may happen in Laying the Levy.

Ordered That Thomas Rice be Levy free

Witneſs John Davis

(76)

At a Veſtry Held for Kingſton Parish at the gleab March 6th. 1770

Preſt. The Rev'd Mr. John Dixon Miniſter Capt Wm. Hayes, Capt Thos Smith Coll. John Peyton Mr George Dudley Mr Edward Hughes Mr Robert Tabb Mr Kemp Whiting

It was agreed to and Signed by the above mentioned Gentm of Veſtry, That the Rev'd Mr John Dixon be absent Some Months and to receive the Rever'd Mr Thomas Baker to officiate for him during his Abſence and to receive the Said Rev'd Mr John Dixon again if it is his deſire to return.

Witneſs John Davis

At a Veſtry Held for Kingſton Pariſh Octobr 29th 1770

Preſent The rev'd Mr John Dixon, The revd Mr. Thomas Baker, Sir John Peyton, Mr William Armistead Churchwd, Major Kemp Plummer, Capt William Hayes, Mr Kemp Whiting, Mr Edward Hughes, Mr Robt Tabb, Captn Frans Armistead, Captn Thomas Smith, & Mr Geo. Dudley

This day The revd Mr John Dixon Reſind the Parrish

It is Agreed to Allow The revd Mr Thomas Baker the Salary or a Proportionable part of it for the time he shall Officiate as Minister of this Parrish and we Agree to Employ him if he Chuses to serve untel a Minister is chosen Allowing him the Uſe of the Gleab and all Other Emolumants the same as to a Rector

Carried up

(77)

The Gent[m] fore mentioned Order that Tobacco be Levied as follows Viz

To The Rev'd M[r] John Dixon 12000	12000 & cask
To Ditto for Shrinkage	480
To Ditto for Quitrents and Acc[t]. £6||5	750
To Capt. John Clayton for Copy of the List Tithables	18
To John Davis Clerk of Church & Veſtry	1700 & cask
To Ditto Sexton of the Old Church	400
To Ditto for taking Care of Church Ornam[ts] Cuſhions &c	200
To D[o] for making Fires in the Veſtry House	100
To Eſtate of Tho[s] Dawſon Deceas'd and Rich[d] Wiatt Royſtone Clerks of the New Church	1200 & cask
To The said Eſtate for keeping the plate	200
To Ann King Sexton of the New Church	400
To Ditto for making Fires in the Veſtry Houſe	100
To Catherine Marwood for keeping Jane Hunley	400
To Mary Bolton Widow	600
To Sarah Baſset Widow	400
To Elizabeth Bridge Widow	600
To Ann Owen Widow for rent	200
To Elizabeth Turner Widow and Children	300
To Judith Machen Widow	300
To Jane Reaves Widow	300
To Suſannah Sadler for keeping her lame Daugh[r]	500
To Richard Morgan and Wife	300
To be left in the Church Wardens hands for Richard Longeſt for keeping Dorothy Parrets Child	1000
To Martha Chriſtian Widow & Children	400
To James Hugget	200
To Deborah Edwards Widow	300
To M[rs] Mary Blacknal for keeping & Colemans Child	400

To D° for ditto omitted Last year	400	
To Ann King Widow & Children	300	
To John Brownley	300	
To John Sampſon	300	
To Elizabeth Brownley Widow & Children	600	
To Joanna Barnet Widow	300	
To Elizabeth Treakle Widow & Children	400	
Carried over	26348	
(78) Acct. Brot over	26348	
To The Rev'd Mr. Thomas Baker Miniſter	4000	& cask
To Ditto for Shrinkage	160	
To Thomas Blake for acct. £7‖12‖6 for work on the Church	915	
To Joſeph King £4‖2‖6 for Horſe Blocks Racks & Coffin	495	
To Capt Shackleford for acct £1‖19‖0½	234	
To Mr Robert Tabb for Inſolvents	512	
To Docr Geo. Johnſon for acct	500	
To Mr Langley Billups for Inſolvents	700	
To Peter Bell for Keeping Thos Crawly having fits	300	
To Richard Morgan & his wife allow'd more	300	
To Richard Parrett for one Levy over paid	25	
To Suſannah Sadler for her Self	300	
To Thomas Newburn for Keeping a Child	100	
To 4 ℔ Ct on 18900 for Cask	756	
	35645	
To 6 pr Ct for Collecting	2138	
	37783	

Ordered That Mr William Smith Sheriff do Receive of Each Tithable Perſon in this Pariſh Twenty six & ½ lbs Tobacco to satiſfy the several Pariſh Creditors

Ordered That Mr John Willis and Capt. Francis Armistead be Church Wardens the Enſuing year

Ordered That the Church wardens do rectify any Miſtake if any is

Ordered That Wm Bridge be levy free

Witneſs John Davis.

(79)

At a Veſtry Held for Kingſton Pariſh Decr 19th 1770

Preſent	Sir John Peyton	Mr Robert Tabb
	Capt. William Hayes	Mr William Armistead
	Mr George Dudley	Capt. Francis Armistead
	Mr Edward Hughes	Mr John Willis
		Gent.m of Veſtry

The Rev'd Mr Thomas Baker, The Rev'd Mr Thomas Field, The Rev'd Mr Arthur Hamilton, and the Rev'd Mr Archibald Avens offering themſelves as Candidates for this Pariſh in the Room of the Rev'd Mr Dixon Reſign'd, and by a Majority of the veſtry the above Mr Field was Choſen whoſe time will Commence from the fifth day of January 1771 The Rev'd Mr Thos Baker having serv'd as Miniſter of this Pariſh according to a former Order of Veſtry three Months.

Test. John Davis

(80)

At a Veſtry Held for Kingſton Pariſh Novr 25, 1771

Preſent, The Rev'd Mr Thos Feilde Minister Sir John Peyton, Capt Thos Smith Mr George Dudley Mr Edward Hughes, Mr William Armistead Capt Francis Armistead, Mr John Willis

Ordered That Tobacco be Levied as follows Viz.

To The Rev'd Mr Thos Fielde Minister	13055¼ & cask
To Ditto for Shrinkage	0522
To The Rev'd Mr Thos Baker	2944¾ & cask
To ditto for Shrinkage	0117
To Mr John Clayton	0018
To John Davis Clk of Church & Veſtry	1700 & cask
To ditto sexton of the old Church	400

To Richard Wiatt Royston Clerk of the New Ch	1200 & cask
To John Davis for keeping Church Ornam[ts] Cushions &c	200
To Ditto for making fires in the Veſtry House	100
To Ann King sexton of y[e] New Church	400
To Ditto for making fires in the Veſtry House at the New Church	100
To Catherine Marwood for keeping Jane Hunley	400
To Mary Bolton widow	800
To Sarah Baſset widow	400
To Elizabeth Bridge widow	600
To Ann Owen	200
To Judith Machen widow	300
To Jane Reaves widow	300
To Susannah Sadler for her lame Daughter	500
To Richard Morgan & wife	600
To Martha Chriſtian widow	400
To James Hugget	300
To Deborah Edwards widow	300
To Ann King Widow & Children	300
To Elizabeth Brownley widow & Children	600
To Joanna Barnet	300

(81)

To acc[t] Bro[t] over	
To Elizabeth Treacle widow & Children	400
To Peter Bell for keeping Thomas Crawley the year past, to be paid to W[m] Smith	500
To Suſannah Sadler for self	300
To Ann Hudgen widow	300
To Sarah Lovet	300
To Robert Keeys for acc[t] £1||3||6	117½
To Margaret Wiatt widow	500
To Tho[s] Blake for work on the Glebe	8000
To Tho[s] Flippen for removing a woman	0100

To Mr John Willis for acct £5‖2‖4	512
To Richard Longest for keeping a Child of Dorothy Parret	500
To Robert Green for 7 Levies over paid last year	183¾
To Sarah Sadler & Children	300
To Mildred Burton for keeping Catherine Ellis's Child	500
To 4 ℔ Ct on 18900 for Cask	756

(82)

At a Veſtry Held for Kingſton Pariſh Novr 25th 1771

Preſent, The Rev'd Mr Thos Feilde Minister
Sir John Peyton, Capt Thos Smith Mr George Dudley Mr Edward Hughes, Mr William Armistead Capt. Frans Armistead and Mr John Willis

Ordered That Tobacco be Levied As follows

To The Rev'd Mr Thos Feilde	13055¼ ca[ ]
To ditto for shrinkage	522
To The Rev'd Mr Thomas Baker	2944¾
To Ditto for shrinkage	117
To Mr John Clayton for Copy of the Liſt	18
To John Davis Clerk of the old Church & Veſtry	1700 & ca[ ]
To Ditto sexton of the old Church	400
To Ditto for keeping Church ornamts Cuſhions &c	200
To Ditto for Making Fires in the veſtry House	100
To Rich'd Wiatt Royston Clerk of ye New Church	1200 & ca[ ]
To Ann King sexton	400
To Ditto for making Fires in the veſtry House	100
To Catherine Marwood for keeping Jane Hunley	400
To Mary Bolton widow	800
To Sarah Baſset widow	400

To Elizabeth Bridge widow	600
To Ann Owen widow	200
To Judith Machen widow	300
To Jane Reaves widow	300
To Suſannah Sadler for her Lame Daugh[r]	500
To Richard Morgan and Wife	600
To Martha Chriſtian widow	400
To James Hugget	300
To Deborah Edwards widow	300
To Ann King widow and Children	300
To Elizabeth Brownley widow & Children	600
To Joanna Barnet widow	300
To Elizabeth trekle widow	400
To Peter Bell for Keeping Thomas Crauley to be paid to W[m] Smith	500
(83)	
To Acc[t] Brought up	27075
To Suſannah Sadler for self	300
To Ann Hudgen widow	300
To Sarah Lovet	300
To Rob[t] Keys for Acc[t] 23/6	117½
To Margaret Wiatt	500
To Tho[s] Blake for work on the Glebe	8000
To Tho[s] Flippen for removing a Woman	100
To M[r] John Willis for acc[t] £5||2||4	512
To Rich[d] Longeſt for keeping Dorothy parrets Child	500
To Rob[t] Green for, 7, Levies overpaid	183½
To Sarah Sadler and Children	300
To Mildred for for keeping a baſtard Child of Caty Ellis's	500
To 4 ℔. C[t] 18900 for Cask	756
	40326¼
To 6 ℔ C[t] Collecting	2419
	42745¼

Ordered That Capt Francis Armistead and Mr John Willis stand Church wardens the Enſueing year

Ordered That Mr Wm Smith receive of each Tithable perſon in this parish thirty two Pounds of Tobacco to sattisfy the several Pariſh Creditors

Ordered That Mr Humphry Gwyn, Mr Thos, Hayes Mr Geo. W^m. Plummer & Mr Gab^l, Hughes Have Notice from the Clerk that they are Choſen Veſtrymen, in the room of Capt. W^m. Hayes Deceas'd M^r. Kemp Whiting, Maj^r Wm Plummer reſign'd & Maj^r Kemp Plummer Deceas'd

Over

(84)

Ordered That Capt Thomas smith, M^r. John Willis, and Sir John Peyton at some at some convenient time meat at the Glebe and view the work done there by Thomas Blake, and order as much of the Tobacco in the Collectors hands to him as they shall think sufficient for the work there done.

Ordered That The Rev'd Mr Feilde have Liberty to diſpoſe or make uſe of such Timber as may be in the Lands if more than he can make uſe of on the Glebe and that the Church wardens acting inspect or looke over the same

Ordered That The depoſ^r in the hands of the Collector be diſpoſed of as the Church wardens may Think Convenient

Ordered That the Gent^m. appointed to view the work done at the Glebe take a Bond of Thomas Blake for his Compleating the work now unfiniſh'd in a reasonable time.

Witneſs John Davis

(85)

[ ] Kingſto[ ]

Nov 28th 1772

Gent^m Preſ^t Sir John Peyton C Thomas Smith M^r. Edw'd Hughes, Mr George Dudley, Mr William Armistead Capt. Francis Armistead, Mr John Willis

Ordered That Tobacco be levied as followeth Viz.

To The Revd Mr Thos Feilde Minis^{r}	16000	& Cask
To ditto for shrinkage	640	
To Capt. John Clayton for Copy list	18	
To Richard. W. Royſton Cl^{k} of the New Church	1200	& Cask
To Ann King sexton of ye new Church	400	
To John Davis Cl^{k} of ye Old Church & Veſtry	1700	& cask
To ditto for sexton of the old Church	400	
To ditto for taking Care of C^{hh} ornam^{ts} & Cuſhions	200	
To ditto for making Fires in the Veſtry House at old C^{hh}	100	
To Ann King for ditto at the new C^{hh}	100	
To Catherine Marwood for Keeping Jane Hunley	400	
To Mary Bolton widow	800	
To Sarah Baſset Widow	400	
To Ann Owen widow for Rent	200	
To Judith Machen widow	300	
To Jane Reaves widow	300	
To Suſanna Sadler for her lame Da^{r}	500	
To Richd Morgan & his wife	600	
To Martha Chriſtian widow	400	
To Deborah Edwards widow	300	
To Ann King Widow and Children	300	
To Richard Morgan toward retrieving his loſs	200	
To Elizath Brownley widow and Children	500	
To Robt Hudgen for Keeping Thos Crauly	500	
To suſanah sadler for her self	300	
To Elizabeth Hudgen	300	
To Thos Flippen for Clearing the Pariſh of Nancy Parret a Bastard Child	500	
	27558	

(86)

[ ]

To Ballance on acc^{t} of Mr John Willis 10/3	68
To Sarah Sadler Widow & Children	500
To Mildred Burton for keeping a Child of	

Caty Ellis	500
To Mrs. Mary Blacknall for Thos Coleman two years	800
To Eliz. Evans widow	300
To Mary Anderton Widow	600
To Ann Fletcher widow	300
To ditto the above 68lb of Mr willis	
To Geo. Willis and his wife	400
To Moſes Hudgen	200
To Dorothy Mullens for Keeping Elz. Snow Longeſt	500
To Ann Longeſt for Keeping Wm Longeſt an Orphan Child	500
To Nicholas Weſcom for taking Nancy Longeſt off the Parish	500
To Edmund Owen for taking Care of in sickneſs and Burying John Davis	100
Allow'd to purchase a Law book	250
To be left in the Collectors hands and apply'd as directed hereafter by the Veſtry	6000
To Capt Francis Armistead for acct for Wine £6	720
To 4 ℔. Ct. on 18900 for Cask	756
	40552
To 6 ℔ Ct. for Collecting	2433
	42985

old orders of Veſtry

(87)

Remainder of orders at the veſtry at the [ ] Church in the year of our Lord 1772 Bro [ ]

Ordered, That Capt Thos Hayes and Mr, Gab[ ] Hughes, stand Church Wardens the Enſueing y[ ]

Ordered That Mr Benjamin Shackelford do Collect of each Tithable Perſon in this Pariſh Thirty fo[ ] and a Quarter

Pounds of Tobacco to satiſfy the severa[ ] Pariſh Creditors

By a Majority of the Veſtry Preſent Mr Walter Keeble, Capt. John Billups and Mr Edmund Cuſtis were Choſen Veſtrymen for this Pariſh

This Day it appearing to the Veſtry the Undernam[ ] Perſons have not given their Liſt of Tithables for the preſent year

Ordered That the Church wardens make Information againſt the s'^d^ perſons, and all others that shall appear to them not to have Given in their Liſts and that this be a standing Rule for the future

Agreed on that the same three Gent^m^ of Veſtry Sir John Peyton Thomas Smith Eſq^r^ and Mr John Willis with Mr Edward Hughes Capt Thomas Hayes and Mr Gab^l^ Hughes do meat at the Glebe or any three of them at some Convenient time and value the work done there by Thomas Blake and Examine his Acc^t^., Likewiſe Examine Likewiſe see what is to do there and have it done

The above Ordres were Signed by the Rev'd Mr Thomas Feilde Miniſter of the above S^d^ Pariſ[ ] of Kingſton

Teſt John Davis

(88)

At a Veſtry Held for Kingſton Parish October 26, 1773

Preſent The Rev'd Mr Thomas Feilde Minister Capt Thomas Smith, M^r^. George Dudly, Mr Edward Hughes, Mr William Armistead, Capt. Francis Armiſtead Capt. Thomas Hayes Mr Gabriel Hughes & Capt. John Billups

To The Rev'd Mr Thos Feild Miniſter	16000
To ditto for Shrinkage 640 To ditto for Cask 640	1280
To Capt John Clayton Cl^k^ of ye County for Copy liſt of Tiths	18
To Thomas Hall Clerk of the New Church	1200
To ditto for Cask	48
To Ann King sexton of the new Church	400
To ditto for making Fires in the veſtry Houſe	100

To Catherine Marwood for Keeping Jane Hunley 400
To Mary Bolton widow 800
To sarah Baſset widow 400
To Ann Owen widow 300
To Judith Machen Widow 300
To Jane Reaves widow 300
To Suſanna Sadler for her Da[r] being lame & havings fits 500
To Richard Morgan & his Wife 600
To Marth Chriſtian widow 400
To Ann King widow & Children 300
To Elizabeth Brownley widow & Children 500
To Robert Hudgen for Keeping Tho[s] Crauley 400
To Suſanna Sadler ℘ self 300
To Elizabeth Hudgen widow 300
To Sarah Sadler widow & Children 500
To Elizabeth Evans widow 300
To Ann Willis Widow 400
To Moſes Hudgen 300
To John Davis Clerk of Church & Veſtry 1700
To Ditto for Cask 68. To ditto sexton 400 468
To ditto for taking Care of C[hh] Ornam'[ts] & Cuſhions 200
To ditto for making Fires in the veſtry Houſe 100
To Mildred Burton for Keeping a Child of Caty Ellis 500
To John Anderton for Keeping an orphan of Mark Anderton 400
To Ann Sellers for two orphans of ditto 800
To Ann Flecher widow & Children 300
To Dorothy Mullins for keeping an orphan of W[m] Longſt 500

31314

(89)

To Acc[t]. Bro[t] over 31[ ]
To Ann Longeſt for an Orphan of W[m] Longeſt Deceas'd 4[]
To Peter Renals for Molly Buſh 4[]

To be sold on the Parish acc[t]	501[]
	37131
To 6 ℘. C[t] for Collecting	2227
	39358

Ordered That M[r] Gabriel Hughes & Cap Thomas Hayes Continue Church Wardens for the ensueing year

Ordered That M[r] Gabriel Hughes or his Deputy do receive of each Tithable person in this Parish twenty Eigh pounds of Tobacco to satisfy the several Parish Creditors there being 1421 Tithables in the List

Ordered That the 5017 lb of Tobacco be Sold by the Collec[r] on July Court day 1774 for this County, in order to Satisfy the Cash acc[ts] as follows

To The Rev'd M[r] Thomas Feild's acc[t] for wine &c	£8 ‖ 18 ‖ 8½
To The Church Wardens ditto	3 ‖ 13 ‖ 6

and for the intended repairs to the Churches and Glebe House

ordered That M[r] Benj[n] Shackelford pay Tho[s] Blake the Ballance of his acc[t] and what remains in his hands to the Church Wardens to be applied to the Cash acc[ts]

Ordered That M[r] William Smith pay the Tobacco remaining in his Hands to Tho[s] Blake

ordered thirty yards of *Crocus for the Parlour at the Glebe

Correct in the above the N[o] of Tithables there being only 1421

Witness John Davis

(90)

[ ] a Vestry Held for Kingston Parish Nov[r] 9, 1774

Present The Rev'd M[r] Thomas Feilde Minister Sir John Peyton, Maj[r] Thomas Smith, M[r] Edw'd Hughes M[r] George

* This word was difficult to decipher. Possibly it has been read wrong.—C. G. C.

Dudley, Capt. Thomas Hayes Mr John Willis Mr Gabriel Hughes Capt John Billups

Ordered That Tobacco be levied as follows

To The Rev'd Mr Thomas Feilde Minister	16000
To ditto for Shrinkage 640 To ditto for Cask 640	1280
To the Clerk of the County for Copy List of Tithables	20
To Thomas Hall Clerk of the New Church	1200
To Ann King Sexton ditto	400
To Thos Hall for Cask	48
To Ann King for Making Fires in the veſtry House	100
To Mary Bolton Widow	800
To Sarah Baſset widow	400
To Ann Owen Widow	300
To Judith Machen widow	300
To Jane Reaves widow	300
To Susanna Sadler for her Dar being lame & having Fits	500
To Richard Morgan & Wife	600
To Martha Chriſtian Widow	400
To Ann King widow & Child	300
To Elizabeth Brownley widow & Children	500
To Suſanna Sadler for self	300
To Sarah S[ ]dler Widow & Children	500
To Elizabeth Evans widow	300
To Ann Willis widow	400
To Moſes Hudgen	500
To Jno Davis Clk of Church & Veſtry	1700
To ditto for Cask 68 To ditto for sexton 400	468
To ditto for taking Care of Church Ornam'ts & Cuſhions	200
To ditto for making Fires in the Veſtry House	100
To Ann Sellers for two Orphans of Mark Anderton	800
To Ann Flecher widow & Children	300
To Dorothy Mullins for Keeping an Orphan of Wm Longeſt	500
To Ann Longeſt for Keeping an Orphan of ditto	400
To Thomas Longest for keeping Molly Buſh	400
To Mary Hudgen Midwife for keeping Thomas Crauley	400
To William Owen	300

To John Purnall for keeping a Child of Caty Ellis	450
To Mildred Burton for keeping a Child of Letty Walſon	400
[ ] Elizabeth Green widow & 4 Children	600
[ ] Thomas Willis for a Child of Dorothy Stedar	400
	32866

(91)

Brough up	32866
To the Eſtate of Maj^r William Plumer Deceas'd for 6 levies overpaid in the year 1773 28 lb of Tobacco each	168
To Mr Ben Shackelford for Isovents this year	620
To Sattisfy the Cash accompts	2000
	35654
To 6 ℔ C^t. for Collecting	2139
	37793
To Ann Longest widow, to be paid out of the Tobacco ariſing from the Concealaled tithables	300

ordered that Capt. John Billups & Maj^r Thos Smith stand Church Wardens the Ensueing year

Mr John Billups Junr do receive of each Tithable Perſon in this Pariſh Twenty eight Pounds of Tobacco to sattisfy the several Parish Creditors

Ordered That the Churchwardens do make information against all those that have not given in their liſts of Tithables, next Court Day

ordered That the 2000 lb of Tobacco levied to pay the Cash acc^ts be sold on July Court Day

ordered that Mr Edward Tabb, & Mr John Dixon have Notice That they are this day Choſen Veſtrymen

ordered

At a veſtry held for Kingſton Pariſh Augt 14, 1775

Preſent Sir John Peyton, Maj^r Thomas Smith, Mr Edward

Hughes, Mr William Armistead, Mr Gabriel Hughes, Capt Thomas Hayes, Capt, John Billups Capt. John Dixon

Agreed that the Church wardens desire Mr Edward Tabb, Mr Ben. Shackelford, Mr Iſaac Smith Mr Wm Smith Mr Matthias James, & Mr John Hunley, Or any three of them to Meet at the Glebe at some Convenient time to view what proportion of Land there appears to have Timbertrees Cut off

(92)

At a Veſtry Held for Kingſton Parish the 11th day of March 1776

Present The Rev'd Mr Thomas Feilde Minis'r Sir John Peyton Majr Thos. Smith Mr Edward Hughes Thos Hayes Gabl Hughes Mr Wm Armistead, & Capt. John Billups

Ordered That Tobacco be levied as follows

To The Rev'd Mr. Thos. Feilde Minister	16000
To ditto for shrinkage 640. To ditto for Cask 640	1280
To the County Clerk for the list	20
To Thos Hall Clerk of the New Church	1200
To ditto for Cask	48
To Ann King sexton	400
To ditto for making Fires in the Veſtry Houſe	100
To Mary Bolton Widow	800
To Sarah Baſset Widow	400
To Ann Owen Widow	300
To Judith Machen Widow	300
To Jane Reaves Widow	300
To Suſanna Sadler for her Daughr being lame & having fits	500
To Richard Morgan & Wife	600
To Martha Chriſtian Widow	400
To Ann King Widow	300
To Susanna Sadler for her self	300
To Sarah Sadler widow & Children	300
To Elizabeth Evans widow	200
To Ann Willis widow	400
To Moſes Hudgin	500

To John Davis Clerk of Church & Veſtry	1700
To ditto for Cask	68
To ditto for for taking Care of Church ornam'ts & Cuſhi	200
To ditto for making Fires in the Veſtry House	100
To	
To Ann Flecher widow & Children	300
To Dorothy Mullins for Keeping an Orphan of Wm Longest	500
To Mary Hudgen Midwife for Keeping Thos Crawley	400
To Wm Owen	300
To Jno Purnall for Keeping a Child of Caty Ellis	450
To Elizabeth Green Widow & 4 Children	600
To Abram Glascock for Keeping Molly Buſh this year	400
To Elizabeth Hudgen for Keeping an Orphan of Mark Anderton	400
To Richd Riſpaſs for 1 of ditto	400
To sarah Weſton Widow	300
To John Elliott for Keeping a baſtard Child of Uſley Davis	150
To Ann Longest widow to pay her Rent	300
To Jno Billups Junr Wine & expence at Williamsburg &c £3||2||6	
(93)	
1776 Acct brot up	
To Ann Longest for Keeping Mary Longeſt @ ye rate of 500lb of Tobo a year	500
To The Rev'd Mr. Thos Feilde for 1 years sacram Wine & 2 Locks £2||13||6	
To Ann Ruff Widow to Pay her Rent	200
To Ann Longest for Keeping Mary Longest some time paſt	300
To Ann Peed for keeping an orphan of Geo. Peed	300
To Sarah Weſton Widow	300
To Wm Foſter for repairs to the old Church £11	
To Docr Edwd Jones for viſit & Medicine for Ann Parrott 19/9	

To The Rev[d] M[r] Tho[s] Feilde for priſing 17280 lb of Toba[o] at 2/6 ℔ Thousand £2||3||2

Ordered That the Church Wardens receive of the late Collec[r] 929 lb[s] of Tobacco & the sum of four Pounds & four Pence to be applied to the Cred[t]. of the Pariſh

To be sold by the Church Wardens at July Glouceſ[r] Court day to satiſfy the several Cash acc[ts] 2000

To 4850 for Collecting @ 14 ℔ C[t]. 4850

Ordered That Maj[r] Tho[s] Smith Collect of each Tithable Perſon in this Pariſh 28 lbs of Tobacco to satiſfy the several Pariſh Creditors

Ordered That M[r] Ben. Shackelford, M[r] George Armistead, M[r] John Hayes & M[r] Rob[t] Matthews Have notice that they are this day Choſen Veſtrymen for this Pariſh

The above Orders of Veſtry were sign'd by the Rev'd M[r] Tho[s] Feilde Minister

Witneſs John Davis

(94)

At Veſtry held for Kingſton Parish April 28th 1777.

Preſent Sir John Peyton Maj[r] Tho[s] Smith, M[r] Edwar Hughes M[r] Gabriel Hughes, M[r] William Armistead, Capt John Billups Cap[t]. John Dixon

Ordered That Tobacco be levied as follows

To The Rev[d] M[r] Tho[s] Feilde Minis[r]	18944
To Ditto for cask 640 To ditto for shrinkage 640	
To which is added for 274 for service till Jan. 1.	1514
for the Liſt of Tithables 2/6 to be p[d] to J. Davis C[k]	
To Tho[s] Hall Clk of y[e] New Church	1200
To Ditto for Cask	48
To Ann King Sexton of the New Church	400
To ditto for making Fires in the Veſtry house	100
To Mary Bolton widow	800
To Sarah Basset widow	400
To Ann owen widow	300
To Judith Machen widow	300

To Jan Reaves widow	300
To Susanna Sadler for her daugh^r being Lame	500
To Richd Morgan & wife	800
To Martha Chriſtian widow	400
To Ann King widow	300
To Susanna Sadler for her self	300
To Sarah Sadler widow & Children	300
To Elizabeth Evans widow	200
To Ann Willis Widow	400
To John Davis Clerk of Church & Veſtry	1700
To ditto for Cask	68
To ditto for taking Care of Church Ornam^ts, & Cuſhi^s	200
To ditto for sexton	400
To ditto for making Fires in the veſtry house	100
To Ann Flecher widow & Children	300
To dorothy Mullins for Keeping an Orphan of Wm Longest	500
To John Purnall for keeping a Child of Caty Ellis	400
To Elizabeth Green widow & Children	600
To Elizabeth Hudgen for Keeping an Orphan of Mark Anderton	400
To Ann Longest to pay her Rent	300
To Ann Ruff widow for ditto	200
To Sarah weston widow	400
To John Elliott for Keeping a Child of Urſly Davis	150
To Dorothy Mullins widow toward paying her rent	200
To Elizabeth Baley	400
To Ann Sellers widow	400
To George Woodin for expence & trouble for Ann Sellers	200
	34424

(95)

Acc^t Brought up	34424
To James Peed for burying Deborah Edwards & expence	250
To Joſeph King for repairing Windows in the New	

Church 8/6

To John Davis serving as Clerk from Octob^r to Jan.	617
To Thos Hall Ditto for Two Months	208
	35499
	2129
	37628

Ordered That Capt Edward Hughes & Mr John Dixon be Church Wardens this year.

Ordered That Mr John Dixon do receive of each Tithable Person 26½ lbs of Tobacco To Satisfy the several Pariſh Creditors and acc^t for the Remainder at the next veſtry

ordered That Mr Dudley Cary have notice that he is Chosen Veſtryman for this Pariſh

The afore said orders were sig'd by Sir John Peyton

Teſt John Davis

(96)

At a vestry Held for Kingſton Parish Feb. 6, 1778

Present Sir John Peyton Mr Edward Hughes Mr Gab^l Hughes Mr William Armistead Capt. John Billups Capt. Thomas Hayes Mr Robert Matthew Mr Dudley Cary

The Rev'd Mr Robert Read & The Rev'd Mr William Dunlop offering Themselves as Candidates for this Pariſh in the room of the Rev'd Mr Feilde *
and by a Majority of the Veſtry the Rev'd Mr R. Read was Choſen

Ordered That The Collec^r pay to each Person the Several sums as follows

To John Davis for being Clerk, Sexton, Making Fires & Keeping Church Ornaments	30	17	0
To Thos Hall Clerk of the New Church 6 Months	7	16	0

* In this space in the MS. there is an asterisk in pencil. At the bottom of page 97 of the MS. a pencilled asterisk occurs again and the words (also in pencil) "who resigned".—C. G. C.

To Ann King Sexton & Making Fires	6	5	0
To Mary Bolton	10	0	0
To Ann Owen	3	15	0
To Susanna Sadler for her lame Daugh[r]	6	5	0
To Richard Morgan & wife	10	0	0
To Ann King	3	15	0
To Susanna Sadler for her self	3	15	0
To Ann Willis	5	0	0
To Elizabeth Green Widow & Children	7	10	0
To Ann Longest for Keeping an orphan Child of Mark Anderton Dec[d]	5	0	0
To Ann Flecher & Children	3	15	0
To Dorothy Mullins for W[m] Longest's orphan	6	5	0
To John Purnal for Caty Ellis's Child	5	0	0
Ann Longest to pay her Rent	3	0	0
To Ann Ruff for Ditto	3	0	0
To John Elliott for John Davis's orphan	3	5	0
To Doroth Mullins to pay her rent	2	10	0
To Elizabeth Baley	5	0	0
To Ann sellers	5	0	0
To M[r] Edw[d] Hughes	1	2	6
To Philip Terrier for Board & Curing Fran[s] Davis Hand	6	0	0
To Ann Longest for Tho[s] Hilling	3	0	0
To John Brownley	5	0	0
	151	15	6
To 6 ℘ C[t] for Collecting	9	4	0
Carried up to the other Leaf	£160	19	6

(97)

1778 The remainder of the order of Veſtry for Feb 6th 1778 Brought up

Ordered That Capt Edward Hughes & M[r] Robert Matthews be Church Wardens the Present year and that Capt. Edward

Hughes Collect from Each Tithable perſon in The sum of Two Shillings & three pence to satisfy the several Creditors

Ordered That Mr Thomas Peyton have notice from the Clerk of the Veſtry that he is this Day Choſen Veſtryman for this Pariſh

The above orders were Signed by Sir John Peyton

Teſt John Davis

(98)

At a Veſtry Held for Kingſton Pariſh Novemr 23. 1778

Present The Rev.d Mr Thos Reade

Sir John Peyton Mr Edward Hughes Mr Gab' Hughes Mr William Armistead Mr John Billups Mr Thomas Hayes Mr George Armistead Mr Dudley Cary

ordered That the Collector pay to each person the several Sums as follows.

	£	s	d
To John Davis Clerk, sexton making fires and Keeping Church ornaments	30	17	0
To John Palister for keeping Geo. Anderton	4		
To Ann Owen widow	5		
To Edwd Hughes	31	15	
To John Peyton	2	8	

Ordered To be entered That The Revd Mr Thos. Reade is choſen & received Minister of this Parish, & that his time began the 14 Day of Augt 1778.

Ordered That Mr Mordicai Throcmortain have notice that he is choſen Veſtryman for this Pariſh

Ordered, That Mr Robt. Matthews & Mr Edwd Hughes be Church Wardens the enſuing year.

Ordered, That Mr Robt Matthews collect from each Tithable Perſon the ſum of twelve ſhillings

Thomas Reade

[The following four-line entry appears on a slip of paper pasted on, and near the bottom of, page 98 of the MS.—C. G. C.]

At a Veſtry Held for Kingston Parish April 10th 1779

Present. Sir John Peyton Maj'r Thos Smith Mr Edwd Hughes, Mr Gabl Hughes Capt. John Billups Mr Geo. Armistead Capt Robt Matthews

(99)
At a Vestry Held for Kingston Parish January 31 1780
Preſent the Rev'd Mr Thomas Read Minister Sir John Peyton, Capt. Edwd Hughes Mr Robert Matthews Mr Gabl Hughes Capt Thos Hayes Capt. John Billups Mr Dudley Cary Capt. Mordecai Throckmorton

Ordered That the Collectr pay to each Perſon the several Sums following viz.

	£		
To John Davis Clerk of Church Vestry &c	112	10	
To Ann King sexton making Fires &c	23	8	9
To Susanna Sadler for her lame Dar	33	15	3
To Richard Morgan & Wife	37	10	0
To Suſanna Sadler for her self	14	1	3
To Ann Willis	18	15	[]
To Dorothy Mullins for William Longests Child	23	8	[]
To John Purnal for Caty Ellis's Child	18	15	[]
To John Palister for Mark Andertons Child & to take it off of the Pariſh	18	15	[]
To Ann Longest for Rent	12	4	[]
To Ann for Ditto	11	5	[]
To John Elliott for Davis's orphan	12	4	[]
To Dorothy Mullins to pay her Rent	9	7	6
To Elizabeth Baley	18	15	0
To Ann Sellers	18	15	0
To Ann Longest for Thos Hillens Child	22	10	0
To John Brownley	18	15	0
To Grace Hudgen for Thomas Newburns son	11	5	0
To Mildred Burton	22	10	0
To Molly Lovet	18	15	0
To James Green to take a Child off the pariſh	22	10	0

To Sufanna Bridges	37	10	0
To Agathy Powers	37	10	0
To Ann Willis	18	15	0
To Ann Atherton	45	0	0
To Elizabeth Brummil for services Done to Thos Newburn & son & Dorothy Bernard	145	10	0
To Capt. Matthews for Wine	78	0	0

for Repairs to the Glebe £500.

Ordered That George Armiftead & Mordicai Throckmorton be appointed Church Wardens

Ordered That James Jones collect from each tithable perfon the sum of twenty fhillings to fatisfy the feveral Creditors as above

Ordered That Philip Tabb be chofen Veftry-Man in the room of Cap[t] Tho[s] Hayes [ ]ho refigns, & Sam[l]. Williams in the room of Dudley Cary who refigns & that [ ] notice thereof

Tho[s] Reade

(100)

Note: This page is blank in the MS.—C. G. C.

(101)

At a Veftry held for Kingston Parish at the old Church the 26th Day of November 1783 Members present, Maj'[r] Thomas Smith, M[r] Edward Hughes, M[r] Gabriel Hughes, Cap[tr] John Billups, M[r] George Armistead, M[r] Samuel Williams, M[r] Armistead Smith, & M[r] Rob[t] Matthews

[ ]der'd Cash to be levi'd as follow's Viz[t].

To Thomas James for Clerk of old Church & Veftry	£ 15	0	0
To for Clerk of New Church	10	0	0
To for Sexton of old Church	2	0	0
To for Sexton of New Church	2	0	0
To Susanna Sadler for self & Daughter	5	0	0
To Richard Morgan	4	0	0
To Dorothy Mullins	1	10	0

To Elizabeth Bailey	1	10	0
To John Brownley	4	0	0
To Ann Owen	1	10	0
To Susanna Terriel	8	0	0
To Judith Mechan	3	0	0
To Wm Baſset Senr for keeping his Siſter Sarah	1	0	0
To Dawson Iddens for keeping Humphry Flippins Child	1	10	0
	60	0	0

[ ]der'd that 5 ℘ Cent be allow'd for Collecting the above, & that Mr Armistead Smith Collect from Each Tithable Person one Shilling to Satisfy the Several Creditors as above

[ ]der'd that the Church Wardens give an Order to the Revd James M.Bride for ten Pounds of the Money they have now to Collect for Rents of The Glebe & hire of the Negroes belonging thereto

[ ]der'd that the Church Wardens Rent out the Glebe & hire out the Negroes belonging thereto for the ensuing Year to the highest Bidder

These above Orders were sign'd by Maj'r Thos. Smith

Teſt Thomas James

(102)

At a Veſtry held for Kingston Parish at the New Church the 28th day 1783, Members present, Sr John Peyton Mr William Armistead, Mr Edward Hughes, Mr Gabriel Hughes, Captn John Billups, Mr George Armistead, Maj'r Mordecai Throckmorton Mr Samuel Williams & Mr Armistead Smith, Gent.

Order'd that Mr Francis Hughes Collect from Each Tithable person 16½d to Satisfy the Several Creditors, directed by Veſtry held the 27th of January laſt

Order'd that he Collect from Mr Hugh Hayse, Mr. Edward Jones, Mr Thomas Gayle, & Maj'r Mordecai Throckmorton

The Tob° due ℘ their Bonds, in the hands of Church Wa[ ] or the value thereof in Cash

The above Orders were Sign'd by Sr Jn° Peyton

Teſt Thos James

Mr Francis Hughes's & his. Father Gabriel Hughes's Bond to the Veſtry

Know all men by these presents that we Francis Hughes & Gabriel Hughes of Kingston Parish in Gloucester County, are held & firmly bound unto the Vestrymen of S^{d} Parish in the just Sum of one Hundred & Eight Pounds Current money of Virginia, which money to be paid to s^{d} Veſtry or their Succeſsors, to the which payment well & truly to be made, we bind ourselves our Heirs & aſsigns, jointly & Severally firmly by these presents, Seal^{d} with our Seals & dated this 28th day of May one thousan[ ] seven Hundred & Eighty three

The Condition of the above obligation is such that if the above bound Francis & Gabriel Hughes or either of them do well & truly Collect from each Tyth[ ] Person within this parish the Several Sums as order'd by Veſtry, and pay the same into the hands of the Church Wardens according to Law, then this Obligation to be void Else remain in full force & Virtue

Francis Hughes (Seal)

Teſt
Thomas James

Gabriel Hughes (Seal)
Copy

(103)

At a meeting of [ ] Church on monday the 27th January 1783 present, Thos Smith Edward Hughes, Gabriel Hughes, John Billups, Geo. Armistead Samuel Williams, Armistead Smith, & Mordecai Throck-Morton Gentlemen Veſtrymen Order^{d} that the Several Sums be paid to the following Persons

	£	s	d
To Thomas James Clark of the Old Church & Veſtry	14	3	4
To Rich[d] Baſset Clark of New Church	10	0	0
To George Woodin Sexton of the Old Church	2	10	0
To William Baſset Sexton of New Church	1	13	0
To Susanna Sadler for Self & lame Daughter	5	0	0
To Rich[d] Morgan	5	0	0
To Dorothy Mullins	1	10	0
To Elizabeth Bailey	1	10	0
To John Brounley	4	0	0
To Ann Owen	2	10	0
To Susanna Terriel	8	0	0
To Judith Machen	3	0	0
To W[m] Baſset Sen[r] for keeping his Siſter Sarah	1	0	0
	59	16	8
Order,[d] that Edw[d] Hurst be exempt from paying Parish levy			
To Dawson Idens for keeping Humphey Flippens Child	1	10	0
To George Armistead for finding neceſsaries for Tho[s] Newbourn & Child	1	15	0
Order,[d] that Samuel Williams & Armistead Smith, Gentlemen be appointed Church Wardens			
To be Deposited in Church Wardens hands	10	0	0
Order,[d] that 5 ℘ Cent be allow,[d] the Church Wardens for Collecting the above	3	13	0
	76	14	8

Order[d] that M[r] Samuel Williams Collect from Each Tithable person the Sum of Sixteen pence farthing to Satisfy the Several Creditors above

To Chr. Pryor for two Copies of Liſts of Tithes 5/

Order[d] that the Church Wardens Collect the Money due for the Rent of the Glebe & Hire of the Negroes

The above Orders Sign'd by Maj^r^ Thos Smith
Teſt Thos James

(104)
[ ] Vestry [ ] 20 [ ]
Present Sir John Peyton Baronet, Major Thomas Smith, Mr William Armistead, Capt John Billup[ ] Mr Robert Matthews, Mr George Armistead, & Maj Mordecai Throckmorton Gentlemen Vestrymen

Ordered that Mr Saml Williams have Notice that he is chosen a Vestryman

Ordered that Mr Thomas Smith and Armistead Smith Ge[ ] have Notice that they are appointed Vestrymen

Ordered that the Revd John Matthews be chosen Minister of this parish in the Room of the Revd Thomas Reade resigne[ ]

Ordered that the Revd Mr Fontaine be requested to prea[ ] once a Month until a Minister resides in the Parish
J Peyton

(105)
At A Veſtry held for Kingston Parish at the old Church August the 19th day 1784 Members present
Maj^r^ Thomas Smith, Mr Wm Armistead. Mr Edwd Hughes, Mr Gabriel Hughes Captn John Billups, Mr Geo. Armiſtead, M^r^. Robt Matthews, Mr Armistead Smith, Captn Thomas Smith Mr Samuel Williams Gen^t^

Ordered The precincts as was laid of in the Year 1780 to stand

Ordered That *Joseph Gayle & Mr Saml Buckner & Mr John Elliot Junr see the proceſsioning of all the Lands within the first precin[ ] perform'd & that †Jno Flipping & Dunkin Glin & Joseph King [ ]ee that the 2nd precinct be proceſsion'd—That Dudley Cary and Richd Gregory, proceſsion the 3rd precinct—

* The words "Joseph Gayle &" scratched through in the MS.—C. G. C.
† The words "Jno Flipping &" scratched through in the MS.—C. G. C.

That Thos Hayes Junr & Josiah Dean proceſsion the 4th precinct —That Holder Hudgin & Ezckiel Lane proceſsion the 5th precinct—That Geo. Gayle, & Thos Tabb proceſsion the 6th precinct That Robt, Billups & Henry Knight proceſsion the 7th precinct That Thos Billups & Joseph Degge Senr proceſsion the 8th precinct.— That James Hunley & Joseph Degge Jnr proceſsion the 9th precinct, That James Thomas & John Armistead proceſsion the 10th precinct, — That James Harper, & Joseph Miller, proceſsion the 11th precinct

Orderd that the Different proceſsioners make a return of their performance according to Law

Orderd, that the Church Wardens make application to the different Debtors for Rents of the Glebe & hire of the Negroes for a final Settlement, & that they make return thereof to the next Veſtry

Ordered that Mr Thomas Tabb be appointed a Veſtry Man & that the Church Wardens acquaint him thereof

Orderd that the Revd, Thomas Hopkinson be receivd as Minister of this Parish, who is hereby authorizd to make use of the Gleb[ ] & other properties belonging to the Church upon Condition that h[ ] faithfully & punctually discharge the Sacred duties & Functions thereof, and abide by any future Determination respecting his *appointment Conduct as the Veſtry shall enter into

Thos: Smith

(106) This page of the MS. is blank.—C. G. C.

(107)

At a meeting of the members of the protestant episcopal Church held on the 28th day of March 1785, it being Monday in Easter Week, I caused to be fairly & duely elected the twelve following Gentlemen, Viz John Peyton, Thomas Smith Senr Edward Hughes, Gabriel Hughes, Robert Matthews, Thomas Smith Junr, Armistead Smith, James Jones, James Booker, Richard Billups, Josiah Deans, & Joel Foster, who are to act as vestrymen for the Parish of Kingston, agreeable to an Act entitled an "Act for incorporating the protestant episcopal Church. Given under my hand the Day & date abovementioned.

Armis[d]: Smith

We the Subscribers, whose names are hereunto annexed, after havi[ ] had it announced to us by the Churchwarden for the Time being, who conducted the Election agreeable to the abovementioned Act, that we were fairly & legally chosen Vestrymen under the same, do hereby solemnly declare that we will be comformable to the Doctrine, discipline & Worship of the protestant episcopal Church, as now incorporated by Law.

Tho[s]: Smith
April 16th 1785 Edw[d]: Hughes

Thomas Smith Jun[r]
Armis[d]: Smith
James Jones
James Booker
Richard Billups
Josiah Deans
Joel Foster
Gabriel Hughes

(108)

At a meeting of the Vestry for this Parrish on the 16th day of April 1785 were present Tho[s]. Smith, Edw[d] Hughe[ ] Tho[s] Smith Jun[r] Armistead Smith, James Jones, James Booker, Richard Billups, Josiah Deans, & Joel Foster, when the following Proceedings were had

Order'd that Tho[s] James be appointed as clerk for the upper & lower Churches & Vestry whose duty it shall be to attend as clerk, the Minister in the discharge of his duty such as reading Psalmody & Burials & also to keep the Vestry Books, & a fair Transcript of their proceedings

Orderd that

Susannah Sadler & Daughter be allowed		£ 9	0	0
Richard Morgan	ditto	5	0	0
John Brownley	ditto	5	0	0
Ann Owen	ditto	1	10	0
Sufannah Terrel	ditto	10	0	0
Dawson Eddins for keeping Hump Flipping Child		1	10	0
Richard Summons & Wife		5	0	0
Elizabeth Jarrot		4	0	0
Order'd that 5 ℔ Ct be allowed		£ 41	0	0
the Collector for Collecting the above		2	1	0
		£ 43	1	0

Order'd that Sir John Peyton & Thos Smith Jr Gen. be appointed Deputes to meet the episcopal Clergy & Vestry in convention to regulate all religious Concerns of the Protestant episcopal Church its doctirns deciplin & Worfhip and to inftitute such rules & regulations as shall be Judged necefsary for the Prosperity & good Government therof

(109)

Order'd that Richard Billups & James Booker be app[ ]ted Church wardens for this Parrish

& that Richard Billups collect Eight pence from each Tithable Person within the sd Parrish & pay the severil [ ] Parrish Poor the fums levied for there Support respective[ ]

Thos: Smith

Note: The rest of this sheet (about four-fifths) has been cut out and removed from the book.—C. G. C.

(110)

This page—or so much of it as remains in the MS. volume (four-fifths of the sheet having been cut out and removed)—is blank.—C. G. C.

(111)

At a meeting of the Veſtry held for Kingston Parish the 14th of November 1786. Preſent Maj^{r} Thomas Smith, Mr Gabriel Hughes, Mr Edwd Hughes, Mr Armis. Smith, M^{r}. James Booker, Mr Joel Foſter, & Capt. Richd Billups

[ ]dered that Capt Richard Billups apply the Money arising for the rent [ ]he Glebe the year 1785 towards furnishing Glaſs for repairing the Church [ ]indows

Orderd that the rev'd James McBride be received as Minister of this Parrish, who is hereby authoriz'd to make use of the Glebe & other properties belonging to the Church upon conditio[ ] that he faithfully & punctually discharge the ſacred duties & function thereof and abide by any futer detirmination respecting his *appointment Conduct as the Vestry ſhall enter into

Order'd posſeſsion of the Glebe be given the Rev'd James McBride on January the 1st. 1787

Order'd that †Sir John Peyton the Rev'd James McBride & Thos Smith Junr Gent^{n} be appointed deputies to meet the episcopal ‡Church Clergy & Vestry in the next convention to regulate all religious Concerns of the Protestant episcopal Church, its doctrine deciplin and Worship and to inſtitute such rules & regulations as shall be Judged neceſsary for the Prosperity & good Government thereof

Thos Smith

(112)

At a meeting of the Veſtry held for Kingston Parish June 6 178[ ]

Preſent, Maj^{r} Thos Smith, Mr Edwd Hughes, Mr Thos Smith jun Mr James Booker, Mr James Jones, Capt. Rich^{d}. Billups & M[ ] Josiah Dean Gen^{t}. Veſtrymen, The following proceeding[ ] were had. This Day the Revd Mr Thomas

* The word "appointment" is scratched through in the MS. and the word "Conduct" written above it.—C. G. C.

† The words "Sir John Peyton" are scratched through in the MS. and the words "the Rev'd James McBride" written above them.—C. G. C.

‡ This word is scratched through in the MS.—C. G. C.

Hopkinson person[ ] came before the Veſtry and made a formal Relinquishment & R[ ]tion of Kingston Parish. —

Order[d] that the Church Wardens [ ] out the Negro Woman Judah. & Rent the Glebe & Glebe Houses untill the first day of January next at publick Auction

Ordered That M[r] Samuel Williams & M[r] Armis[d] Smith former Church Wardens be Summoned to make return to the next Veſtry of the Debts due the Parish for Rents & Negro hires according to a former order dated August 19th 1784

Tho[s]: Smith

(113)

At a meeting of the members of the Protestant Episcopal Church held on the 17th. of July 1787. I caused to be fairly and duly elected the twelve following Gen[t]., Viz, Sir John Peyton, Thomas Smith Armistead Smith, George Armistead, Thomas Smith Jun[r]. James Booker, Dudley Cary, James Jones, Edward Hughes, Joel Foster, Thomas Tabb, and Robert Cary, to be Vestry and Trustees of their property, agreeable to an Ordinance of Convention held in the city of Richmond on the 16th of may 1787

James Booker, C. W.

We the subscribers whose names are hereunto annexed, after having it announced to us by the Church Warden for the tim[ ] being, who conducted the Election agreable to the above [ ]-tioned Ordinance, that we were fairly and legally cho[ ] Vestrymen, and Trustees under the same do hereby solemnly declare that we will be conformable to the do[ ]trine discipline and worship of the Protestant Episcopal Church

July 24th 1787

Tho[s]. Smith
Armis[d]: Smith
Geo Armistead
Thomas Smith Jun[r]
James Booker
Ja[s] Jones
Edw[d]: Hughes

Joel Foster
Rob[t] Cary
Thomas Tabb

(114)

At a meeting of the Vestry, and Trustees, for Kingston Parish had at the Glebe on the 24th of July 1787, were present

Thomas Smith, Arm[d] Smith, George Armistead, Thomas Smith Jun[r], James Booker, James Jones, Edw[d] Hughes, [ ]oel Foster, and Robert Cary. the following proceedings [ ]ere unanimously agreed to

Ordered — That Thomas Smith and Edward Hughes be appointed Church. Wardens

Order'd, that the Church Wardens forthwith make application to M[r] Sam[l] Williams, M[r] Arm[d] Smith, M[r] Rich[d] Billups former Church . Wardens, and M[r] Francis Hughes Collector of this parish to account for the several Bonds taken and deposited in their hands for the rents of the Glebe or hire of Negro's

Ord[d] That the Church. Wardens contract with any person or persons for the neceſsary repairs of the Churches and Glebe

Ord[d] That the said Church . Wardens, apply such Bonds as they may receive, or the money ariseing there-from or any part thereof towards making such repairs, and make return of their proceedings to the next Vestry

It being suggested and represented that trespaſses have bin made upon the Lands belonging to the Glebe and Churches, Ord[d] that the Church . Wardens do take such steps as they may deem most proper to prevent the said practice, by aſcertaining the boundaries and quantity of said Glebe Lands; as well as [ ]ose heretofore appropriated for the Churchyards & [ ]ing Grounds

(115)

Ord[d] That Thomas Smith Jun[r] Gen[t]. be appoint[ ] a Deputy to meet the Episcopal Clergy and Laity in Convention to regulate all religious conc[ ] of the Protestant Episcopal Church, its doctrin[ ] discipline and Worship, and to institute suc[ ] rules and regulations as shall be juded neceſ[ ]ry for the prosperity and good government thereof

Thos: Smith

At a meeting of the Vestry & Trustees for Kingston Parish, held at old Church June 19th 1788. Present Revd James McBride, Thomas Sm[ ] Armd Smith, George Armistead, James Booker, Edwd Hughes, Joel Fo[ ] Thomas Tabb & Robt Cary, the following proceedings were agreed to

Orderd on report of the Church Wardens, that they have made application to the difft Debtors for the sevl sums due for Rents of Glebe & Hire of [ ] & that their Application proving unsucceſsfull, the repairs of Churches & Glebe hath not bin complyed with

Ordd That the sevl Bonds due the Church be entered on the Book; [ ] are as follows

Doctr Edwd S Jones Dr. a Bond given the 1st day of Jany 1783 for 3500 T[ ] payble on Demd wth Intt from the date for Rent of Glebe 1782

To 1 years Rent for 1783 Mr Saml Williams C. W. £18.0.0 no Bond taken

To a Bond given for Rent of yr 1784—dated Decr. 16th 1783 payble ye Ensuing [ ]

Dr Majr Mord. Throckmorton. To a Bond given for 1400 wt of Tobo date [ ] the 21st day of August 1784 payble 20th Novr followg

Dr Thomas Gayle To 2 Bonds given Jany 1st. 1783 one for £6||10||0 the other for 750 wt Tobo = To a Bond given Decr 16th 1783 for 30 / payble the ensuing year

Anty. Gautier Dr To a Bond given June 20th. 1785 for £6||10||0 pay[ ] Jany 1st 1786

To a Bond given Decr 1st 1785 for £36||12||0 payble Jany 1st 1787 R[ ] Matthews & James Hunley Securities

Ordd that the Church Wardens make application for payment [ ] the above Bonds, & if not immediately discharg'd, to Commence Suit

(116)

that [ ] his Acc. for Repairs [ ] the Glebe amounting to £3||2||9 wth Int[t] from the 26th day of March 1787

[ ]rd that James Booker be appointed Treasurer.

[ ]d[d] That Thomas Smith Jun[r] Esq[r] be appointed a Deputy to meet the Episcopal Clergy & Laity in Convention to regulate all religious concerns of the Protestant Episcopal Church, its doctrine discipline & worship [ ] to institute such rules & regulations as shall be judged neceſsary for the prosperity & good Government thereof

Ja[s] M[c]Bride

At a Meeting of the Vestry for Kingston Parish, held at the Croſs Roads on the 19th Day of August 1792. When were Present Thomas Smith, George Armistead, Thomas Smith Jun[r] James Jones, Joel Foster, Thomas Tabb, & Robert Cary, which appearing to be a Majority, the Vestry proceeded to adopt the following Orders.

Ordered that M[r] Thomas Smith be authorized to act as Clerk of the Vestry for the Day

This Day the Rev[d] Armistead Smith produced to the Vestry Testimonials of his [ ]piscopal Ordination, which being deemed proper & satisfactory; Ordered, that the s[d] Rev[d] Armistead Smith be received into the Parish of Kingston, as their Pastor [ ] Minister, that he be permitted to officiate therein as such, & authorized to enjoy all [ ]he Rights, privileges & advantages, which a Pastor can enjoy or exercise, under the Rules, & Canons of the Protestant episcopal Church.

Ordered that the Rev[d] Armistead Smith be served with the Order afores[d] & that he be requested to give his attendance on the Vestry

Present the Rev[d] Armistead Smith

Ordered that M[r] Dudley Cary, M[r] Richard Gregory, M[r]

John Cary, Mr Josiah Foster, & Mr Milton L. Glaſsock, be appointed Members of this Vestry, to act as such, untill the next triennial Election, & that it be accord[ ]gly announced to the Gentlemen aforesd by the Clerk

Ordered, that Mr Richard Gregory be appointed a Church Warden in the Room of Mr Edward Hughes decd & that it be announced to [ ].

(117)*

That they have a high Sence of his steady attachment to the true Interest of the protestant Episcopal Chur[ ] of his Fitneſs & Abilities to take upon himself the impor[ ] Duties of his office; of the Integrity, the Industry, orderly & exemplary Conduct, with which he has discharged th[ ] & when the Orders of a Priest shall be confirred [ ] him, they hereby expreſs their Willingneſs to receive, [ ] & encourage him as their Pastor & Minister

Ordered that the said Revd Armis[ ] Smith be & he is hereby warmly recommended to [ ] Right Revd James Madison Bishop of the Protesta[ ] Episcopal Church of Virginia, as a Person in their [ ]inion capable in all Respects of hischarging the im[ ]tant & Sacred Duties of a Minister; that as such [ ] acquitted himself with Fidelity, Circumspection, and [ ]nce; with undoubted Attachment to the Prosperity of the Church, of which he is Minister; & merits in the Opinion of the Vestry the Approbation & highest Reward of a grateful People in the Discharge of the many laborious, interesting, & sacred Duties which are instan[ ] to his office

John Cary Clk Ves[ ]

(118)

Note: This page in the MS. is blank.—C. G. C.

* By mistake the leaf containing the pages of the MS. at present numbered 117 and 118 was, at some time when the MS. was rebound, inserted here. Obviously it should have been inserted after the leaf containing the pages now numbered 119 and 120.—C. G. C.

(119)

Ordered that the Rev[d] Armistead Smith be requested to in[ ] M[r] Thomas James to return to our Parish, & act as Clerk to [ ] Churches; & that he aſsure him that the Vestry will exert the [ ] to promote his Interest as such, as well as in teaching Psal[ ] adjourned

Armis[d] Smith

Test
Thomas Smith C. V.

* At a Meeting of a Vestry for Kingston Parish held at the New Church on t[ ] Day of Septem[r] 1792, when were present the Rev[d] Armistead Smith, Thomas Smith, George Armistead, Thom[ ] Smith Jun[r] James Jones, Joel Foster, Thomas Tabb, Rob[t] Cary, Rich[d] Gregory

At a Meeting of a Vestry for Kingston Parish, held at the New Church on the 21st Day of Septem[r] 1792. when were Present the Rev[d] Armistead Smith, Thomas Smith, George Armistead, Thomas Smith Jun[r] James Jones, Joel Foster, Thomas Tabb, & Robert Cary which appearing to be a Majority, the following Proceedings were entered into.

This day M[r] Richard Gregory, M[r] John Cary, & M[r] Milton L. Glaſsock gave the [ ] attendance, & were duly qualified to act as Vestrymen untill the next triennial Electi[ ]

Ordered That the Rev[d] Armistead Smith be Put in Poſseſsion of the Glebe house & Lands on the 1st Day of Jan[y] 1793 to be made use of & enjoyed by him as the Minister of this Parish.

Ordered, that the Churchwardens do furnish out of the Means now in their Hands, fine Hollan[ ] for two Surprices for the use of their Minister.

The Vestry having nothing farther to delivered on, Ordered that it be now adjourned

Armis. Smith

* This entry is half erased in the MS., but is still legible.—C. G. C.

(120)

[ ] Meeting of the Vestry for Kingstone Parish held at [ ]oſs Roads on the 27th day of March 1793

When were Present Thomas Smith Senr Thomas Smith Junr George Armistead Robert Cary Richard Gregory Dudley Cary and John Cary which Appearing to be a Majority the Vestry Proceeded to Adopt the following Orders

Ordered That The Revd Armistead Smith and Dudley Cary Esquire be Appointed Deputys to meet the Episcopal Clergy & Laity in Convention to regulate all Religious concern of the Protestant Episcopal Church its doctrine discipline & Worship & to institute such rules & regulations as shall be judged nece[ ]ary for the Prosperity & Good Government thereof

Ordered That Thomas James be appointed Clerk of the upper and Lower Church and that he have notice thereof as this day Elected by the Vestry and that it be recommended to him to send forward Subscriptions to enable him to do the duties thereof

Armisd Smith

At a Vestry held in Kingstone Parish in the County of Mathews on the 27th day of July 1793 When were present the following Members Viz The Revd Armistead Smith Thomas Smith Junr Robert Cary George Armistead Richard Gregory and John Cary

Ordered that it be announced to the Revd Armistead Smith by the Churchwardens of this Parish that the Vestry are duly impreſsed with a Recollection of the Singular Services, which he has Rendered both to the Church in its collective Capacity, as well as the Individuals of our Parish in the faithful Discharge of the sacred Functions of a probationary Minister in Deacons Orders;

(121)

At a Meeting of the Vestry for the Parish of Kingst[ ] in the County of Mathews the 13th day of May 1796

When were present the following Members Viz The Rev[]

Armistead Smith Thomas Smith Sen[r] Thomas Smith [ ] Richard Gregory Francis Armistead John Patterson Ja[ ] Van Bibber John Cary & Sands Smith We the under W[ ] Vestrymen & Trustees do oblige ourselves to be conforma[ ] to the doctrin disciplin and Worship of the Protest[ ] Episcopal Church in the United States of America and to the Orders & Cannons of the said Church in this [ ]

Armistead Smith Min.
Thomas Smith Sen[]
Thomas Smith Ju[ ]
R. Gregory
James V. Bibber
Francis Armistea[ ]
Sands Smith
John Cary

Ordered That Thomas James be appointed Clerk [ ] Lower Church as also Clerk of the Vestry for this [ ]

Ordered that Thomas Smith Jun[r] & John [ ] be Appointed Church Wardens for this Parish [ ] as such till the next Trianual Election

Ordered that the Rev[d] Armisted Smith & James V. [ ] Esquire be Appointed Deputys to meet the Episcopal Cle[ ] & laity in Convention to be holden at Richmond in [ ] next to regulate all Religious concerns of the Protesta[ ] Episcopal Church its Doctrin disciplin & Worship & to [ ]-

(122)

stitute such rules & regulations as shall be Judged neceſ[ ] for the Prosperity & good Government thereof

Ordered that Thomas Smith Sen[r] & Rich[d] Gregory Esq fo[ ]mer Church Wardens of this Parish Meet the Next Vestry [ ]Settle & Acc[t]. for all Money that may have come into their hands for the use of the Churches

Ordered that John Patterson Esq[r] be requested to purchase a Record Book for the use of the Church & that Rich[d] Gregory

Esq[r] late Church Warden be requested to [ ] With him for the same

The Vestry being informed that John Patterson Esq[r] [ ] fuses to Subscribe as Vestryman agreable to his Election

Ordered that Rich[d] Wiatt be appointed Vestryman [ ] this Parish in his stead & that the Clerk make known [ ] the said Wiatt his s[d] Appointment

[ ]dered that Francis Armistead be Appointed Tresurer [ ] this Parish

Armistead Smith Minis.

John Cary Clk Protem

At a Court held for Gloucester County the 5. day of Feb[y] 1784

Ordered that the Vestry of Kingston Parish in this County divide the said Parish into so many precincts as to them shall ſeem most convenient for proceſsioning every persons Lands within the said Parish and appoint particular times between the last day of March next and the last day of September following when the proceſsioning shall be made in every precinct and also appoint two intelligent Honest freeholders of every precinct to see the Proceſsioning perform'd and to take and return to the s[d] Vestry an Account of every persons land th[ ] proceſsion and of the persons present at th[ ] and of what lands in their precinct they sha[ ] proceſsion and of the particular reasons for [ ]

Copy. C. Pry[ ]

Note: The above entry—which sufficiently explains itself—was written upon a scrap of old laid paper, six by eight inches, which was later pasted upon a sheet of ordinary, modern white paper, six by ten inches. It was found lying in, but not attached to, the Kingston Parish Vestry Book.—C. G. C.

APPENDIX

APPENDIX

CLERGYMEN

The following list contains the names of the ministers (Incumbents of the Parish and temporary supply preachers), who served, or were elected to serve, Kingston Parish between 1680 and 1796. The numeral (in parentheses) preceding the clergyman's name indicates the number of the page on which the name first appears. The date (in parentheses) following the name indicates the year in which the clergyman's name is first mentioned in this book.

(2)	Zyperus, Mychaell (1680)
(7)	Boker, James (1690)
(23)	Blacknall, John (1740)
(40)	Dickson, John (1749)
(41)	Locke, Richard (1749)
(43)	Dixon, John (1750)
(91)	Baker, Thomas (1770)
(94)	Feilde, Thos. (1770)
(110)	Read, Robert (1778)
(112)	Reade, Thos. (1778)
(115)	McBride, James (1783)
(118)	Matthews, John (1783-4)
(118)	Fontaine (1783-4)
(119)	Hopkinson, Thomas (1784)
(122)	McBride, James (1786-elected)
(126)	Smith, Armistead (1792)

The following list contains the names of clergymen who offered themselves unsuccessfully as candidates for the Incumbency of Kingston Parish:

(94) Baker, Thomas (1770)
(94) Hamilton, Arthur (1770)
(94) Avens, Archibald (1770)
(110) Dunlop, William (1778)

CLERKS OF THE VESTRY

The following list contains the names of the Clerks of the Vestry of Kingston Parish between 1679 and 1796:

(2) Axe, George* (1679)
(13) Bolton, Henry (1701)
(24) Brookes, Wm. (1740)
(44) Davis, John (1750)
(114) James, Thos. (1783)
(126) Smith, Thos. (1792)
(127) Cary, John (1793)
(130) James, Thos. (1796)

PHYSICIANS

The following list contains the names of the physicians mentioned in this book:

(28) Roche (1742)
(29) Symmer, John (1743)
(42) Whiting, Peter (1750)
(50) Asselin (1753)
(81) Johnson, George (1765)
(90) Clayton, Thos. (1769)
(107) Jones, Edw. S. (1776)

* With regard to George Axe it is interesting to note that in 1671 a man of the same name was serving as "Reader" (Clerk) of Pyanckatancke Church in the neighboring Parish of Christ Church, Middlesex County, and that from this date until Nov. 5, 1678, he seems to have served as clerk in two or three other churches and chapels in the parish. After 1678 his name appears no more in the Christ Church Parish records. See *The Vestry Book of Christ Church Parish, Middlesex County, Virginia,* 1663-1767.—C. G. C.

List of Subscribers

List of Subscribers

American Antiquarian Society, Worcester, Mass.
Anderson, Mrs. Jno. F., New Brunswick, N. J.
Baker & Taylor Co., New York, N. Y.
Bell Book and Stationery Co., Richmond, Va.
Bell, Landon C., Columbus, O.
Bryan, John Stewart, Richmond, Va.
Bussey, Mrs. Arthur, Columbus, Ga.
Cary, Hunsdon, Richmond, Va.
Chandler, R. G., Chicago, Ill.
Cincinnati Public Library, Cincinnati, O.
Columbia University Library, New York, N. Y.
Daughters of the American Revolution Library, Washington, D. C.
Detroit Public Library, Detroit, Mich.
Eggleston, Dr. J. D., Hampden-Sydney, Va.
Embrey, Alvin T., Fredericksburg, Va.
Goodspeed's Book Shop, Boston, Mass.
Gordon, Armistead C., Staunton, Va.
Gordon, James W., Richmond, Va.
Gray, W. Palmer, Richmond, Va.
Grinnan, Daniel, Richmond, Va.
Hampden-Sydney College Library, Hampden-Sydney, Va.
Handley Library, Winchester, Va.
Harris, John T., Harrisonburg, Va.
Harrison, Fairfax, Washington, D. C.
Hill, Walter M., Chicago, Ill.
Indiana State Library, Indianapolis, Ind.
Iowa Historical, Memorial & Art Department, Des Moines, Iowa.
James, Mrs. Geo. N., Petersburg, Va.
Jones Memorial Library, Lynchburg, Va.
Jones, T. Catesby, New York, N. Y.
Kansas State Historical Society, Topeka, Kans.
Klemen, Mrs. J. G., Jr., Haverford, Pa.
Library of Congress, Washington, D. C.
Long Island Historical Society, Brooklyn, N. Y.
Los Angeles Public Library, Los Angeles, Cal.
Massachusetts Historical Society, Boston, Mass.
Michael, C. Edwin, Roanoke, Va.
Milwaukee Public Library, Milwaukee, Wis.
Minnesota Historical Society, St. Paul, Minn.
Missouri Historical Society, St. Louis, Mo.
Mitchell, Edwin Valentine, Hartford, Conn.
Morse, Mr. V. D., Ithaca, N. Y.
McFall, James, Pittsburgh, Pa.
McNeill, Mrs. W. S., Richmond, Va.
Nebraska State Library, Lincoln, Nebr.

Newberry Library, Chicago, Ill.
Newport News Public Library, Newport News, Va.
New York Public Library, New York, N. Y.
Norfolk Public Library, Norfolk, Va.
North Carolina State Library, Raleigh, N. C.
Ohio Historical and Philosophical Society, Cincinnati, O.
Payne, John Barton, Washington, D. C.
Peabody Institute, Baltimore, Md.
Pennsylvania Historical Society, Philadelphia, Pa.
Quinn, Mrs. J. J., Houston, Texas.
Ramsdell, Chester H., Point Independence, Mass.
Rowland, Dr. Dunbar, State Historian, Jackson, Miss.
Smith, H. M., Jr., Richmond, Va.
Stewart, Misses Lucy and A. C., Brook Hill, Va.
St. Louis Mercantile Library, St. Louis, Mo.
Stone, Miss Lucie P., Hollins College, Va.
Taylor, Mrs. Henry, Jr., Richmond, Va.
Tennessee State Library, Nashville, Tenn.
Texas University Library, Austin, Texas.
Tyler, Dr. Lyon G., Holdcroft, Charles City Co., Va.
University of Virginia Library, University, Va.
Virginia Historical Society, Richmond, Va.
Virginia State Library, Richmond, Va.
Western Reserve Hist. Society, Cleveland, O.
West Va. Dept. Archives and History, Charleston, W. Va.
William and Mary College Library, Williamsburg, Va.
Wood, Mrs. Wm. P., Richmond, Va.

INDEXES

Index of Names of Persons

* See note on p. 136.

Geographic Index

Topic Index

www.ingramcontent.com/pod-product-compliance
Lightning Source LLC
Chambersburg PA
CBHW071125280326
41935CB00010B/1113

* 9 7 8 0 7 8 8 4 1 3 2 3 0 *